24 GREAT walks in EDINBURGH

Author: Richard Jones
Managing Editor: Apostrophe S Limited
Series Editor: Donna Wood
Art Editor: Andrew Milne
Copy Editor: Stephanie Smith
Proofreader: Jackie Staddon
Picture Researcher: Lesley Grayson
Production: Stephanie Allen
Image retouching and internal repro: Sarah Montgomery

Edited, designed and produced by AA Publishing.
© Automobile Association Developments Limited 2009

Published in the United States by
Wiley Publishing, Inc.
111 River Street, Hoboken, NJ 07030

Find us online at Frommers.com

Frommer's is a registered trademark of Arthur Frommer.
Used under license.

Cartography provided by the Mapping Services
Department of AA Publishing

Enabled by [Ordnance Survey] This product includes mapping
data licensed from the Ordnance
Survey ® with the permission of the Controller of Her
Majesty's Stationery Office. © Crown copyright 2008.
All rights reserved. Licence number 100021153.
A03625

ISBN 978-4704-5372-8

A CIP catalogue record for this book is available from
the British Library.

Colour reproduction by Keene Group, Andover
Printed in China by Leo Paper Group

OPPOSITE: ROSS FOUNTAIN IN PRINCES STREET GARDENS

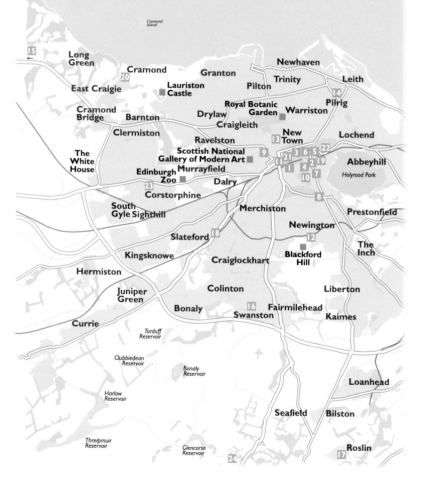

Firth of Forth

Cramond Island

Long Green

Cramond

Granton

Newhaven

Trinity

Leith

East Craigie

Lauriston Castle

Pilton

Pilrig

Cramond Bridge

Barnton

Drylaw

Royal Botanic Garden

Warriston

Clermiston

Craigleith

New Town

Lochend

Ravelston

The White House

Scottish National Gallery of Modern Art

Abbeyhill

Holyrood Park

Edinburgh Zoo

Murrayfield

Corstorphine

Dalry

South Gyle

Sighthill

Merchiston

Prestonfield

Slateford

Newington

The Inch

Kingsknowe

Blackford Hill

Hermiston

Craiglockhart

Juniper Green

Colinton

Liberton

Bonaly

Fairmilehead

Swanston

Kaimes

Currie

Torduff Reservoir

Clubbiedean Reservoir

Bonaly Reservoir

Harlow Reservoir

Loanhead

Threipmuir Reservoir

Glencorse Reservoir

Seafield

Bilston

Roslin

CONTENTS

Introduction

Edinburgh is one of the most beautiful and striking cities in Europe and is a wonderful place to explore on foot. Built on seven hills, overlooked by an extinct volcano, and dominated by its castle, Edinburgh looks more like a theatrical backdrop than a modern city, and the casual wanderer who strays from the busy well-trodden thoroughfares will find much that is fascinating. One of the most intriguing things about Scotland's capital is that it has two distinctive sections, the Old Town and the New Town.

The Old Town is dominated by its castle, perched on a volcanic mass of basalt rock and visible from many of Edinburgh's streets. From it stretches the Royal Mile, an avenue connecting the castle to Holyrood Palace and along which the people of Edinburgh conducted and still go about their daily business. Leading away from this throbbing artery are lots of minor streets, known as *closes* and *wynds*, and it was here that daily life went on with rich and poor crammed side by side, or, since the tenements in which they lived stretched heavenwards, on top of and below each other. The New Town was begun in the 18th century and comprises stunning buildings, glorious crescents and the largest area of Georgian architecture in Europe.

Edinburgh is also an incredibly countrified capital and, within a few strides of its bustling centre you encounter glorious glens, picturesque riverside walks and, of course, the splendid wilderness of Holyrood Park around Arthur's Seat. There are also villages to explore that, although once remote outlying enclaves, have now been absorbed into the urban spread of an ever expanding city.

In this book you will find 24 walks that capture the essence of Edinburgh. They take in the well-known and well-trodden tourist spots, but they also include many places that are off the beaten track. If time is an issue and you can only do a handful of the walks then walks 1 and 2 are recommended, as they cover the Royal Mile and can be combined to make one longer walk. To get an in-depth feel for the New Town try walk 21.

However, the book is made up of lots of different areas and provides the opportunity to experience some of the lovely countryside and mysterious places outside Edinburgh.

Chief amongst these is the village of Roslin, home of the stunning Rosslyn Chapel, which achieved a new lease of international fame when author Dan Brown featured it in his best-selling novel, *The Da Vinci Code*. Particularly recommended is the walk that takes in the site of the Battle of Rullion Green, both for its glorious countryside and its turbulent history.

The walks are not just about events and people, however, for each one has been carefully paced out to create an intriguing combination of atmospheric routes and interesting places to look at. Limited space has meant that not every point of interest – in a city that teems with them – could be included. But that doesn't mean that you won't encounter them. So look out for the information boards that provide details on other sites not included and inspect the many statues that you will pass by which remember famous and the not

so famous figures featured in the story of Edinburgh. Take a breather to admire the houses and absorb the character of the neighbourhoods explored and let those narrow and mysterious wynds and closes become doorways of discovery.

In short, be sure to take your time and explore every twist and turn encountered. Absorb the ambience of the variety of neighbourhoods through which you will pass. But above all else, enjoy the histories and ponder the mysteries that have, quite literally, been written on the streets through which you're walking.

WHERE TO EAT

£	=	Inexpensive
££	=	Moderate
£££	=	Expensive

ABOVE: DUSK OVER PRINCES STREET

Dark Deeds and Dark Shadows in Old Town

This walk is crammed with history and every corner you turn presents a new surprise to wonder at. The perfect introduction to the Royal Mile.

Since this walk begins outside Edinburgh Castle, you might like to start by visiting it. Having done so, set off on your journey along the first section of the Royal Mile, the long spine that stretches from the Castle to Holyrood Palace and is in fact a little over a mile long. The walk proper will take you in and out of the closes (the term commonly used to describe a narrow passage between houses) and wynds (wider passages into which a small cart could fit) that lead off the Royal Mile and where the everyday life of the Old Town went on. Many of the closes have information boards at their entrances, which tell historical stories and facts. In addition you will pass by many other closes that, although not featured on the walk, are still worth venturing into to absorb their ambience. Although several interiors are mentioned that are not open in the evenings, this walk is a spooky night-time roam and so you might like to return after dark.

With your back to the Castle, walk forward and pause to the left, just before the Tartan Weaving Mill. On the wall here is the Witches Fountain, designed by John Duncan in 1894 and erected in 1912 to commemorate the 300 unfortunate souls who were burnt as witches on Castlehill between 1492 and 1722. Opposite to the right is Castle Wynd North and, having descended the first steps, take a look up at the middle window.

A little way up from its right corner a small cannon ball can be seen embedded in the wall, which gives the 15th-century tenement building its name – Cannonball House. Tradition has it that the cannon ball came to be embedded in the wall after it was fired from Edinburgh Castle towards Holyrood Palace, where Bonnie Prince Charlie had taken up residence during the Jacobite uprising of 1745. The truth turns out to be a little less dramatic: it was in fact placed here as a marker to indicate the maximum gravitational height of the first piped water supply to the city.

2 Backtrack and head right along Castle Hill, passing the Tartan Weaving Mill to your left.

This was formerly the water tank built in 1850 to store the city's water supply. Keep ahead along the right side of Castle Hill, passing on your right The Scotch Whisky Experience, which tells the story of Scotland's staple beverage and where you can, if you wish, enjoy a wee dram

WHERE TO EAT

|O| DEACON'S HOUSE,
3 Brodie's Close, 304 Lawnmarket;
Tel: 0131 226 1894.
Atmospheric little café offering wholesome home-made fare. £

|2| THE HALFWAY HOUSE,
24 Fleshmarket Close;
Tel: 0131 225 7101.
This genuinely old-fashioned pub has occupied its site in Fleshmarket Close since the 18th century and was once surrounded by abattoirs and butcher's shops. It is a freehouse that offers a selection of beers and the usual pub food. £

to steady your nerves for the dark wynds and closes that lie ahead!
THE SCOTCH WHISKY EXPERIENCE;
www.whisky-heritage.co.uk

3 Go left along Ramsay Lane where on the right is the entrance to the Outlook Tower and Camera Obscura.

It's well worth climbing the tower via a sequence of rooms with a variety of puzzles and optical illusions to mull over up to the highlight – the Camera Obscura, installed in 1853 by Edinburgh optician Maria Theresa Short. It uses a system of lenses and mirrors to beam images from the streets below onto a viewing disc. It might be a little voyeuristic, but it is great fun watching unsuspecting pedestrians going about

9

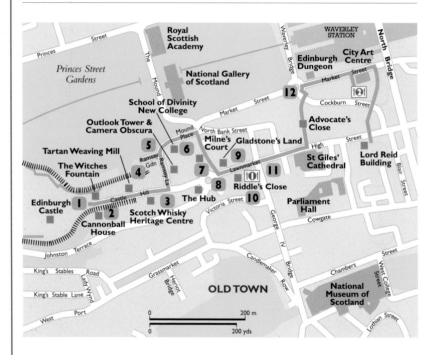

their business oblivious to the fact that their miniature selves are being made to climb over hurdles (well white pieces of card) by those in the viewing chamber.

CAMERA OBSCURA;

www.camera-obscura.co.uk

4 Continue down Ramsay Lane and go first left into Ramsay Garden. The rambling and half timbered buildings ahead were constructed by Sir Patrick Geddes (1854–1932) and completed in 1894. Keep going ahead.

Note the two dragon supports high up on the right wall, and pause in the courtyard. To your right are the remaining pilasters of the octagonal Ramsay Lodge, built by the 18th-century poet Alan Ramsay for his own use around 1740 and known as Goose Pie House because of its unusual shape.

5 Backtrack and go left along Ramsay Lane. As the decline levels off, pass the line of lamps and benches and then go right through the gates to enter the

10

courtyard of the world-renowned School of Divinity New College, part of the University of Edinburgh.

It shares its site with the General Assembly Hall, the main meeting place for the Church of Scotland. A full history of the buildings can be seen on the wall to your right as you enter. In the courtyard to the left is a bronze statue of John Knox dating from 1895.

6 Backtrack through the gates, turn right, following the railings as they curve right until you see a formidable flight of stone steps ahead of you. Climb them to reach Milne's Court.

Amazingly atmospheric, imbued with a darkly sinister ambience, Milne's Court was built by Robert Mylne (or Milne) in the late 17th century. The buildings were restored to provide student accommodation in 1969.

7 Exit Milne's Court onto Lawnmarket where, to your right, is the former Highland Tolbooth St John's Church – now the Hub. This historic Pugin building has been transformed into a café and restaurant.

The building is one of the most prominent landmarks on Edinburgh's City Skyline. It was designed by Augustus Pugin and James Gillespie and constructed between 1842 and 1845, not as a church but as the Assembly Hall for the Church of Scotland. It is now the headquarters of the Edinburgh Festival.

8 From Milne's Court go left along Lawnmarket and, a little way along, turn left into James' Court West Entry, another dark and dingy place redolent with the chill of Edinburgh's murky past. Bear right and, just by the door of 7a, go sharp right to pass the lounge bar entrance of the Jolly Judge Pub, keeping ahead through the dark passage. Exit left along Lawnmarket, and two doors down on the left is Gladstone's Land.

Named after Thomas Gladstone, who bought the property in 1617, this restored tenement is now owned by the National Trust for Scotland and has been restored to provide visitors with the opportunity to get a real feel of what it was like to live in Old Town Edinburgh 400 years ago. It is only open in the summer.

9 Exit Gladstone's Land, cautiously cross to the other side of Lawnmarket and go through the gates into Riddle's Close, which is in fact two picturesque courtyards.

In the second one is a house built around 1592 by Baille Macmorran, noteworthy for its peculiar outside wooden staircase on the left, once a common feature of Old Town properties. As town baille, Macmorran was responsible for enforcing law and order and, on the morning of 15 September 1595, he was called to a disturbance at the old High School, where several boys had barricaded themselves in as a protest against a reduction to their holidays. As his officials began battering down the door, Macmorran was shot and killed by William Sinclair, son of the Chancellor of Caithness. Sinclair's family connections ensured that the boy only spent a short time in prison for his crime.

10 Backtrack, go right along Lawnmarket and take the second right into Brodie's Close. A little way along is Deacon's House.

Now a pleasant little café, Deacon's House was once the cabinet-making workshop of the father of William Brodie (1741–1788), one of Edinburgh's most infamous rogues. Having followed his father into the cabinet-making trade, Brodie became a much-respected figure in Edinburgh society, so much so that he was elected Deacon Councillor of the City in 1781. But Brodie's respectable façade hid a dark side. Using his daytime trade to acquire knowledge about the security mechanisms of his wealthy clients, he would also take wax impressions of their keys, make duplicates and then burgle their houses by night. Brodie was finally brought to justice and hanged at Edinburgh's Tolbooth in 1788 on the City's new gallows, which, ironically, he is reputed to have helped design.

11 Go left over the traffic lights and turn right in front of Deacon Brodie's Tavern. You can read more of the infamous Deacon Brodie's story on a brass plate on the wall. Keep ahead over Bank and St Giles streets onto High Street and, just past No. 361, go left into Advocate's Close.

This steep, narrow thoroughfare dates from around 1544. Its antiquated feel soon gives way to modern buildings, but you really do feel that you've been transported back into Edinburgh's distant past.

12 At the end of the close, go right through the passage and at the bottom of the steps cross over Cockburn Street. Bear left then right along Market Street, on the opposite side of which is the Edinburgh Dungeon. Continue, passing the City Art Centre, after which go right to ascend the steps of Fleshmarket Close. There follows a long climb past two old pubs, the Half Way House and Jinglin Geordie. Keep ahead over Cockburn Street into Jackson's Close. At the end cross High Street, bear right on its other side and go left into New Assembly Close, which leads to the Lord Reid Building.

This splendid Georgian structure was built in 1814, and makes for a fitting end to an intriguing walk.

13

Beyond the World's End

From the Tron Kirk to Holyrood Palace, this walk cuts a swathe through some of the Old Town's most evocative closes and fine historic buildings.

This is a truly eventful stroll along a fascinating section of the Royal Mile. It goes in and out of the closes and uncovers some of the older properties that lie behind the modern façades. It begins with a walk down one of Edinburgh's more chilling streets before passing a 16th-century mansion that is now a youth hostel. Having learnt the story of a famous 19th-century disaster, you have the opportunity to come face to face with the great Scottish reformer John Knox. Moving on, you pass the site of the place that for many centuries was, quite literally, the end of the world for the majority of Edinburgh's citizens. Having stepped past it you head along Canongate, where you can visit two of the Old Town's free museums. Having stood by the grave of a famous 16th-century murder victim, you have the opportunity to explore an idyllic secret garden, before passing the controversial buildings of the Scottish Parliament to end your walk outside Holyrood Palace, to which you might wish to pay a visit.

1 With your back to Tron Kirk turn right and cross South Bridge. Take the first right into Niddry Street. Pause on the right outside Nicol Edwards, which proclaims itself to be Scotland's most haunted pub. At the end of Niddry Street head left along Cowgate, then left into Blackfriars Street, once known as Blackfriars Wynd.

Here, on April 30th 1520, the rival clans of the Douglases and the Hamiltons fought a pitched battle that went down in history as 'Cleanse-The-Causeway' because of the amount of blood that had to be cleaned up afterwards.

2 Ascend the left side of Blackfriars Street and pause outside the doorway of the High Street Hostel, formerly Morton House and originally constructed by James Douglas, 4th Earl of Morton (1525–1581), who acted as Regent of Scotland during the minority of James VI and who was beheaded on Edinburgh's 'Maiden', a guillotine-type device that he himself had introduced into Scotland. Keep ahead, cross over High Street, bear right and pause a little way along on the left by Paisley Close.

Look up at the stone face of a boy above its entrance over which are the words 'Heave awa' chaps, I'm no dead yet'. On 24 November 1861 a tenement building that stood on this site suddenly collapsed, killing 35 people. As the rescuers clawed at the debris they heard a faint voice calling pathetically from beneath the rubble, 'Heave awa' lads, I'm no dead yet.'

Digging down, they were able to rescue a young boy named Joseph McIver, whose image is now carved above the arch along with his cry.

3 Keep straight along High Street and pause outside John Knox's House.

John Knox's House is open to the public and contains an exhibition dedicated to the famed Scottish reformer, although it is uncertain whether he ever had any actual connections with the building. Also note Moubray House to its left. These are among the oldest houses in Old Town, dating from the latter part of the 16th century.

4 Continue along High Street and cross it just after the Scottish Storytelling Centre. Keep ahead through the archway into Tweeddale Court, where you will come to Tweeddale House.

E 1 mile (1.6km)

hour 20 minutes

START Outside Tron Kirk

FINISH Holyrood Palace

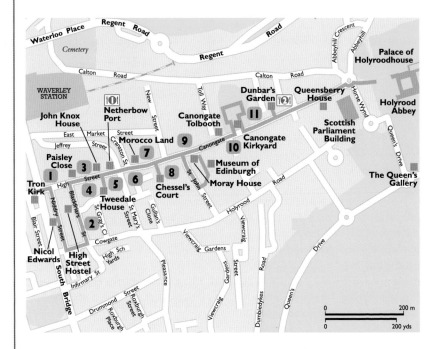

The house was built around 1600 and became the town house of the Marquess of Tweeddale in 1670. By the 19th century it had become the headquarters of the British Linen Bank. At around 5pm on 13 November 1806, bank porter William Begbie was found lying in the passage through which you have just walked. He had been stabbed with a knife which was still embedded in his chest. The unfortunate Begbie was beyond help and he died a little while later. The motive for his murder was evidently

robbery as £4,392 that he had brought from the bank's branch in Leith was missing. Despite the fact that some of the money was later recovered, the crime has never been officially solved.

5 Backtrack and go right along High Street. At the traffic lights, note the brass plaques in the roadway at the junction with St Mary's Street.

These plaques mark the location of the Netherbow Port, a massive gateway

16

demolished in 1764 through which people once passed in and out of the City. As this was where Edinburgh ended, for the majority of its citizens this spot was, quite literally, the end of their world and it thus became known as World's End, a name still commemorated by the World's End pub just before the traffic lights. A brief history of the area can be read on the wall of the pub.

6 Cross over St Mary's Street into Canongate, once the thoroughfare by which the Augustinian Friars travelled between their monastery at Holyrood and the City of Edinburgh.

Because it was outside the confines of the cramped city, Canongate became a desirable place to live, and its proximity to the Royal Court at Holyrood made it popular with nobles, who built their mansions along what was for centuries an independent burgh in its own right. When you arrive at Gullan's Close look over the road where a statue of a Moor adorns the façade of Morocco Land. It commemorates Andrew Grey, who, according to legend, broke out of prison on the eve of his execution in 1633 and fled to Morocco. Here he became immensely wealthy and in 1645 he returned to Edinburgh determined to take his revenge. However, he arrived during one of the worst outbreaks of plague in the town's history. Having taken the Provost's daughter hostage, he managed to cure her of plague, promptly fell in love with her and then married her. Deciding to spare the town but

unable to settle there as he had taken a vow never to set foot in Edinburgh again, the couple moved into a house on Canongate, where he later placed this statue of the emperor of Morocco.

7 Continue and go right into the attractive Chessel's Court with its fine Georgian architecture.

Directly in front of you is an impressive block of mansion flats built in 1748 as accommodation for the town's middle classes. It was in Chessel's Court that the General Excise Office for Scotland once stood and which Deacon Brodie and his gang attempted to rob on 5 March 1788. The failure of this burglary forced Brodie to flee Edinburgh for Holland from where he was brought back, tried and executed.

8 Backtrack to Canongate, turning to the right to see the external stone balcony of Moray House at No. 174.

In 1650 the Marquis of Montrose passed this way en route to his execution in the Lawnmarket. Looking up he saw the smiling face of his arch adversary, the Earl of Argyle, who was attending the wedding of his son to the Earl of Moray's daughter. Argyle ordered the cart to stop and spat contemptuously into Montrose's face.

9 Keep ahead, crossing to the left side of Canongate and pause outside the Canongate Tolbooth.

The Tolbooth was built in 1591 and was the administrative centre of the

Canongate when it was an independent burgh. It was also its courtroom and jail. The building now houses the People's Story museum that, along with the Museum of Edinburgh opposite, tells of the life and times of local inhabitants.

PEOPLE'S STORY/MUSEUM OF EDINBURGH;

www.cac.org.uk

10 Continue along Canongate and into Canongate Kirkyard.

The handsome striding statue to the right of the gate is of the poet Robert Fergusson (1750–1774). His poem *Auld Reekie* (Old Smoky) vividly portrays the sights, sounds and smells of an Edinburgh long gone. You can find his grave if you pass to the left of the church and turn left just after the grave of Peter Lyle. Fergusson was confined to an asylum, committed suicide and was buried in a pauper's grave. Poet Robert Burns was so incensed by the lack of a memorial to Fergusson that he paid for the headstone and composed the epitaph. Backtrack, pass to the left of the church and keep straight through the two gateposts. Bear right on arrival at the boundary wall, passing three huge memorial stones and pause at the next grave along, which bears the name Clarinda. This is the

ABOVE: STATUE OF POET FERGUSSON OUTSIDE CANONGATE CHURCH

grave of Nancy Craig, with whom Robert Burns carried on a passionate correspondence in which he signed himself Sylvander and she signed herself Clarinda. Burns later wrote his loveliest lyric, *Ae Fond Kiss*, for her. Continue along the path, follow it as it bears right towards the church and pause just before the Kirk's first and second windows. The battered grave by the wall is reputedly that of David Rizzio (1533–1566) Italian musician and personal secretary to Mary, Queen of Scots. He was stabbed to death in front of her on 9 March 1566 by a group of nobles that included Mary's husband Lord Darnley. Tradition maintains that his grave was moved here from Holyrood in 1688.

11 Exit the gates, go left along Canongate, then left into Dunbar's Close. Pass through the gate into lovely Dunbar's Garden, laid out in 17th-century style. Backtrack, continue left along Canongate, cross to its right side, and continue until, just after the bus stop, pause by the gates of Queensberry House, before reaching the modern Scottish Parliament building.

The house was built in 1682 by William, 1st Duke of Queensberry. The 2nd duke was one of the prime movers behind the Union of the English and Scottish parliaments in 1707. His son was reputedly mentally unstable and was kept hidden away in a secret room in the house. On the day that the Union was ratified his son's keeper left the room to watch the riots in Canongate,

WHERE TO EAT

[1] THE WORLD'S END,
41 High Street;
Tel: 0131 556 3628.
This atmospheric, snug little hostelry is something of an Edinburgh institution. With a dark wood interior and low ceilings, it offers hearty meals that include steaks, pies, the inevitable haggis, tatties and neeps. The only downside is that it can get very busy. ££

[2] CLARINDA'S TEA ROOMS,
69 Canongate;
Tel: 0131 557 1888.
This traditional and very cozy tearoom is a pleasant place to stop at. The tables all have lacy tablecloths and patterned china lines the walls. Light meals, sandwiches and afternoon teas are offered, as well as a selection of goodies such as cakes, shortbread, rock buns and apple pies. £

and returned to find the duke's son crouched by the kitchen fire roasting the kitchen boy on the spit. Next door is the new Scottish Parliament designed by the Spanish architect Enric Miralles (1955–2000.) The building was three years late in opening and, famously ended up costing over 10 times its original estimated budget of £40 million. Keep ahead to the Queens Gallery of Holyrood Palace.
SCOTTISH PARLIAMENT;
www.scottish.parliament.uk

BENJAMIN WEST'S *DEATH OF THE STAG* (1786) AND SCULPTURE IN THE NATIONAL MUSEUM OF SCOTLAND

Art and Artefacts

Although not a particularly long walk, from a historical and cultural perspective it visits some of Scotland's top museums and galleries.

Beginning with the Scott Monument, an iconic Edinburgh landmark that dominates Princes Street, you then move on to explore the galleries and enjoy the artworks displayed within the National Gallery of Scotland. From there you trudge up the Mound to visit a museum that is dedicated to money and has several fascinating tales to tell. Speaking of tales, your next stop is the Writers' Museum, located inside a 17th-century mansion and dedicated to Scotland's three greatest authors – Burns, Scott and Stevenson. A few short strides and you find yourself entering the hallowed portals of the National Library for Scotland, where you have the opportunity to step back in time. Finally, you cross the threshold of the National Museum of Scotland, which takes you on a spellbinding, often thrilling journey through Scotland's rich and diverse history. The walk can be as short or as long as you like, its duration determined by how long you spend at each gallery or museum.

1 Start the walk by the Scott Monument in Princes Street.

When Sir Walter Scott died in 1832 it was decided that a fitting monument to his memory should be erected, and in 1836 an architectural competition was launched, inviting designs for a suitable memorial. The winning design was submitted by George Meikle Kemp. Construction was completed in 1846, since when millions of visitors have made the ankle-jarring climb up its 287 stairs to enjoy the views from the top of this 200ft-high (60m) Gothic marvel. Tragically Kemp never lived to see his masterpiece completed, as he was drowned one foggy night in the Union Canal (see Walk 11). At the centre of the monument you will see a large seated figure of Sir Walter Scott together with his favourite pet dog, Maida. Characters from his novels and famous figures from Scottish history also adorn it at various levels.

SCOTT MONUMENT;

www.cac.org.uk

2 With your back to the Scott Monument, go left along Princes Street and turn left just before the Royal Scottish Academy.

The Royal Scottish Academy building was designed by William Henry Playfair (1790–1857) and opened in 1826. It originally housed the Society of Antiquaries and the Royal Society but was converted in 1911 to become the headquarters of the Royal Scottish Academy. The building's exterior is grand indeed and is surmounted by a statue of the young Queen Victoria. Initially this stood at street level but the Queen was reputedly not amused by her chubby appearance so she ordered it to be placed at roof-top level to avoid more close examination by her subjects.

ROYAL SCOTTISH ACADEMY;

www.royalscottishacademy.org

3 Keep ahead then turn right. Immediately on the left is the entrance to the highly regarded National Gallery of Scotland.

The gallery is another Playfair building that opened to the public in 1859. It is a truly magnificent place and its lavish interior has the feel of a stately home. Its galleries boast a magnificent collection of European paintings and sculpture from

23

DISTANCE 1 mile (1.6km)

ALLOW 2–3 hours including visits to the museums and galleries

START The Scott Monument on Princes Street

FINISH The National Museum of Scotland

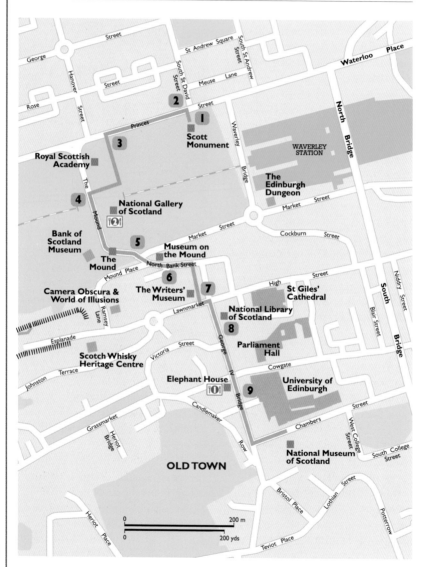

the Renaissance to Post Impressionism. The Scottish Galleries contain works by Sir Henry Raeburn, including his 'Skating Minister', more properly *The Reverend Robert Walker Skating on Duddingston Loch*, one of Scotland's best-known artworks.

4 Exit left out of the gallery, turn left again, and ascend the steep incline of Anchor Street up onto The Mound.

This artificial hill was created from the earth dug out for the foundations of the New Town houses and buildings, and was said to consist of two million cartloads of soil. Another name for it was 'Geordie Boyd's Mud Brig', after George Boyd, an Old Town tailor who had many clients in the New Town and who constructed a track made of planks and stones over the earthen mound to create a short cut to his customers.

5 Cross over Market Street, and go left through the gates to enter the Museum on the Mound.

The museum is housed in part of the Bank of Scotland building, constructed in 1806 and remodelled by David Bryce in the 1860s to create the exquisitely grand building that greets you today. The museum is both fun and fascinating – there's a lot more to money and banking than you'd suppose. Inside you can see a million pounds; wonder at Scotland's oldest banknote and even try your hand at cracking open a safe.

MUSEUM ON THE MOUND;

www.museumonthemound.com

6 Leave the bank, go right out of the gates and veer left over the pedestrian crossing, then bear left along North Bank Street. Turn right through the gates and carry on to ascend the steps of Lady Stair's Close. On the right is The Writers' Museum, located in Lady Stair's House.

Built in 1622, the initials of the original owner, William Grey of Pittendrum, and his wife, Geida Smith (WG and GS), can be seen carved over the door along with the words 'Feare The Lord and Depart From Evil'. Grey installed an intriguing anti-burglar device inside whereby one of the stairs is a different height to the others. This was intended to trip any intruder moving around the house in the dark. The building and the close are named for Lady Stair, who bought the house in 1719. It now contains The Writers' Museum, dedicated to three of Scotland's most famous writers – Robert Burns, Sir Walter Scott and Robert Louis Stevenson. In the basement room, dedicated to Stevenson, is a cabinet made by the infamous Deacon Brodie (see Walk 1), which was in Stevenson's bedroom when he was a child.

THE WRITERS' MUSEUM;

www.cac.org.uk

7 Leave the museum and head straight on. Go up the steps and turn left along Lawnmarket. Keep ahead over Bank Street and go right on its other side to cross Lawnmarket and keep ahead onto George IV Bridge. On the left is the National Library of Scotland.

Go inside and turn right to enter the John Murray Archive.

John McMurray established the publishing house of John Murray in London in 1768. Over the next seven generations, from its headquarters in Albemarle Street, it evolved into one of the world's greatest publishers and still exists now as part of French publishing giant Hachette. In 2002 John Murray the seventh offered the firm's archive to the National Library of Scotland, and part of that collection is now displayed in this permanent and imagination-firing exhibition. With display cases dedicated to individual authors – including Lord Byron, Charles Darwin and Thomas Carlyle – and a layout that literally transports you back in time.

JOHN MURRAY ARCHIVE;

www.nls.uk

8 Leave the Library and go left along George IV Bridge, cautiously crossing it via the bollards, and turn left along its other side. Just after the Central Library, pause and look down at Cowgate far below. Edinburgh is a city of bridges and it is at spots like this that you realize how often you are walking high above its true level. Continue and pause outside The Elephant House café on your right.

This Edinburgh institution is popular with just about everyone. It oozes atmosphere and its back room affords a spectacular view of Edinburgh Castle. It is also one of the cafés in which author, J K Rowling wrote the early chapters of her mega-successful Harry Potter stories.
THE ELEPHANT HOUSE;
www.elephant-house.biz

9 Cautiously cross to the left side of George IV Bridge, turn next left into Chambers Street and turn right immediately over the crossing. Ahead of you is the National Museum of Scotland.

The building's style of architecture caused controversy from the outset and Prince Charles resigned as patron of the museum protesting that too much weight had been given to the opinion of 'so-called experts'. It opened to the public in 1998 and, despite Prince Charles' refusal to comment on the building when he visited it that year, in 1999 it won the Best Building of the Year prize awarded by the Royal Fine Art Commission Trust. This state-of-the-art museum tells the

WHERE TO EAT

⒯ THE ELEPHANT HOUSE,
21 George IV Bridge;
Tel: 0131 220 5355.
The Elephant House bills itself as 'The Birthplace of Harry Potter', because this is where the author J K Rowling often 'mulled over a coffee writing her first Harry Potter novel'. Good views, good food and great coffee. £

⒲ THE GALLERY RESTAURANT AND BAR,
National Gallery Complex
The Mound;
Tel: 0131 624 6580.
Sandwiches and coffees are available in one section, with full meals such as roast breast of wood pigeon or homemade fishcakes offered in the restaurant. All food is freshly prepared using local ingredients. ££

story of Scotland from the geological dawn of time to the modern day, and among the exhibits are Dolly, the cloned sheep and the Hunterston Brooch, an exquisite piece of jewellery dating from around AD700. You can also view eight of the 17 miniature coffins found in 1836 in a cave on Arthur's Seat (see Walk 22). The Royal Museum next door can be reached by a connecting walkway; this soaring Victorian structure, completed in 1888, is undergoing a £46 million renovation due to be completed in 2011.
NATIONAL MUSEUM OF SCOTLAND;
www.nms.ac.uk.

Hangings, Murders and Witchcraft

This walk begins with a visit to one of Edinburgh's most intriguing historic sites and then journeys through the darker side of Edinburgh's history.

The walk includes several interiors, so is best done between 9.30am and 4pm when they are open to the public. It begins with a visit to Parliament Hall, a lovely old building that few visitors venture inside. The next interior is St Giles' Cathedral, which really does have the mark of history upon it. From here you move on via tales of executions and witchcraft to the district where the Burke and Hare murders occurred between 1827 and 1828. There then follows a walk past one of the best preserved sections of Edinburgh's historic Flodden Wall, to enjoy a magnificent view of Heriot's School before encountering an atmospheric old chapel. Having explored several closes that give a vivid idea of what it was like to live in the Old Town in days gone by, you emerge onto the busy High Street to end your journey at the Real Mary King's Close, an underground section of Edinburgh that is steeped in legend.

I Begin at the Mercat Cross, once a gathering place for merchants.

This was also the spot from which proclamations were read and where executions were carried out. Today guided tours of Edinburgh gather here and proclamations are still read out. Legend holds that on the night before the Battle of Flodden in 1513 a ghostly herald appeared at the Mercat Cross and was heard reading out the ill-fated names of all those who were destined to die in the bloody battle.

2 Walk to the left of the Mercat Cross and head across the cobblestones of Parliament Square. Go past the barrier and walk over to the statue of King Charles II, which dates from 1685 and is both the oldest statue in Edinburgh and one of the oldest equestrian lead statues in Britain. Pass to the left of the statue and pause on car park bay 23.

Here an orange square marks the grave of the great reformer John Knox. He was buried in the churchyard of St Giles' Cathedral but this was later paved over, leaving him at rest beneath a parking lot.

3 Bear left and go in through the doors of No. 11 to enter and see the striking interior of Parliament Hall.

In the hall look up at the magnificent hammerbeam roof, made of Danish oak and installed in 1639. Prior to 1707 and the union of the Scottish and English

parliaments, this was the meeting place for the Scottish Parliament. It is now part of Scotland's supreme criminal and civil court and you will see bewigged counsel and solicitors pacing back and forth discussing cases in low voices.

4 Exit Parliament Hall, cross to St Giles' Cathedral and enter via the left door. Look up at the window on the left, designed by the Pre-Raphaelite artist Sir Edward Burne Jones and made by William Morris in 1886. With your back to the window, climb the steps and pause to admire the statue of John Knox (1505–1572), who spent 12 years as the church's minister. Just past the statue go left into the chapel.

The recumbent figure you see is Archibald Campbell, Marquis of Argyle. The Marquis was beheaded on 27 May 1661 for his part in the earlier beheading of the Marquis of Montrose, leader of Charles I's forces in Scotland, who was executed at the Mercat Cross on 21 May 1650. His dismembered remains were finally laid to rest on the opposite side of the cathedral in 1661 on the orders

OPPOSITE: STAINED GLASS WINDOW IN ST GILES' CATHEDRAL DEPICTING JOHN KNOX

DISTANCE 1.75 miles (2.8km)

ALLOW 1 hour 15 minutes

START Mercat Cross

FINISH The Real Mary King's Close

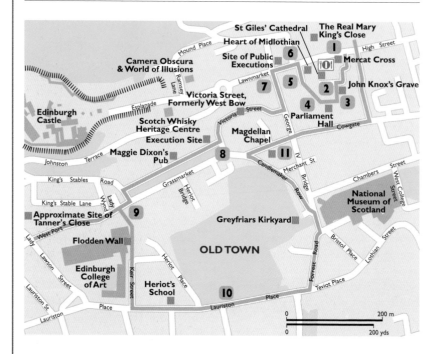

of Charles II. Exit the chapel and go left, turning right past the stone pulpit then turn left at the next column. On the right is the Thistle Chapel, the chapel of the Knights of the Thistle, an order of chivalry which consists of the Sovereign and 16 Knights and Ladies, all of whom join by the monarch's own personal invitation. Leave the Thistle Chapel, head left through the two columns and swing immediately right to enter the next chapel on the left. On the left is the memorial to James Graham, Marquis of Montrose

(1612–1650), who is buried here. Exit the chapel, turn left and keep ahead past the organ. Just after the small brown wooden pulpit, and a little way past the radiator, a small plaque commemorates Janet Geddes (1600–1660), who near this spot is reputed to have thrown her stool at the head of the minister as a protest at the introduction of the Anglican Book of Common Prayer in Scotland. A modern re-creation of the stool is on display.

ST GILES' CATHEDRAL

www.stgilescathedral.org.uk

5 Exit the Cathedral, turn right off the steps and just by the road pause at the cobblestones, which are shaped to form a heart motif.

This is the Heart of Midlothian, which marks the site of the Old Tolbooth Prison demolished in 1817. It was here that Captain Porteous was imprisoned after being sentenced to death for ordering his men to fire on the stone-throwing crowd following a public execution in Grassmarket in 1736. He was later reprieved, which didn't go down too well with the Edinburgh mob, who stormed the Tolbooth, dragged him to the Grassmarket, and hanged him from a dyer's pole. It is customary to spit on the cobbled heart as a gesture of contempt to the memory of the old prison. On the railing to the left is an information board giving a full history of Parliament Square and its surroundings.

6 Continue over the Heart of Midlothian and keep ahead past the Lawnmarket Well.

On the corner by the lights there is a wall plaque commemorating the last public execution in Edinburgh, that of George Bryce, which took place on 21 June 1864. The site of the gallows is marked by three brass plates set into the pavement at the edge with the road.

7 Cross George IV Bridge via the crossing that bears left and take the first right down Victoria Street, formerly known as West Bow.

One of the most famous residents of West Bow was Major Thomas Weir (1599–1670), an esteemed preacher and epitome of puritanical respectability. It therefore came as something of a shock when, at the age of 70, the major suddenly confessed to being a warlock and admitted a string of terrible offences including bestiality, necromancy and incest with his sister, Jean. The two of them were executed in 1670 and his bizarre double life reputedly became one of the inspirations for Robert Louis Stevenson's *Dr Jekyll and Mr Hyde*.

ABOVE: HEART OF MIDLOTHIAN

8 At the foot of Victoria Street go right onto Grassmarket and cross to the railings that surround the execution site where around 100 Covenanters died for their faith between 1661 and 1688. Keep ahead, passing Maggie Dixon's pub on the right. On the wall you can read the full story of Half-hangit Maggie. Continue over Castle Wynd South, passing the White Hart Inn, once a favoured haunt of the notorious 19th-century murderers, Burke and Hare. Follow Grassmarket as it bears left and pause at the junction with West Port. If you wish you can turn right and walk up to its junction with Lady Lawson Street by the traffic lights.

This was the approximate site of Tanner's Close, infamous as the residence of Burke and Hare, who, between 1827 and 1828, murdered around 17 men and women and sold their cadavers to the university's lecturing anatomists. Burke was hanged in the Grassmarket on 28 January 1829 and his body was handed over to the anatomists for dissection. Hare turned king's evidence and was later released, although he had to flee Edinburgh for fear of mob reprisals. Here you pass an impressive section of the Flodden Wall.

9 Cross over West Port, bear left on its other side and turn right to ascend the steps of Vennel.

The wall was built to defend Edinburgh against a threatened English invasion in the wake of the Battle of Flodden (1513) at which James IV of Scotland was killed.

Continue to the end and go left along Lauriston Place, passing Heriot's School on the left. A board to the right of the main gate provides a brief history.

10 Continue and, at the traffic lights go left along Forrest Road. You might like to make a detour and visit Greyfriars Kirkyard on the left (see Walk 10), otherwise veer left along Candlemaker Row, keep ahead over Merchant Street and go right along Cowgate. A little way along on the right is the Magdellan Chapel, built in 1541.

This church boasts four stained-glass windows dating from the mid-16th century, the only complete stained-glass window in the whole of Scotland. It is open Monday to Friday 9.30–4.

11 Exit the chapel, go right along Cowgate, cross to its left side and pass through the arch of George IV Bridge. Just before the coloured columns supporting a modern building go left along Old Fishmarket Close. Just before the green boxes go up the steps of Barrie's Close on the left, follow it as it bends right and turn right into Parliament Square. Keep ahead over High Street, go left in front of City Chambers and next right into Warriston's Close. Ahead is The Real Mary King's Close.

This is an intriguing warren of hidden closes in which you can experience the sights and sounds of the street that time forgot.

THE REAL MARY KING CLOSE;
www.realmarykingsclose.com

33

EDINBURGH'S NATIONAL PORTRAIT GALLERY

Medics, Murder and the Real Sherlock Holmes

Edinburgh's New Town is a World Heritage Site and its streets encompass the buildings and statues of those who helped shape modern Edinburgh.

By the mid-18th century overcrowding in Edinburgh's Old Town had reached breaking point and the city fathers became anxious to create a New Town that would reflect the Age of Enlightenment and the modern thinkers to whom Edinburgh had become home. In 1766 a competition was held to select a design for this modern metropolis and the winner was 23-year-old James Craig, who proposed two large squares connected by three parallel streets. The plan was intended to be symbolic of the equal partnership between Scotland and England, following the Union. Thistle Street and St Andrew's church would represent the former, whilst Rose Street and St George's church would represent the latter. The New Town was constructed in stages and completed in 1850. The historical figures encountered include the real-life Sherlock Holmes, a notorious 19th-century murderer, a pioneering doctor and, inevitably, the man who truly helped put Scotland on the literary map, Sir Walter Scott (1771–1832).

1 Start at the equestrian statue of the Duke of Wellington on Princes Street.

The statue dates from 1848 and was the work of Sir John Steell. The curious thing about it is that the entire weight of the duke and most of that of the horse is borne by the horse's rear legs. The secret, apparently, is in the tail, which is crammed full of lead as a counter-balance.

2 With your back to the statue, go right along Princes Street, take the first right into West Register Street and keep ahead along Gabriel's Road to the right of the Guildford Arms. Having passed the Café Royal, turn left, go first right into Register Place, and pass through the gate in its far left corner. Descend the steps, turn right, and go right through the doors of Dundas House, completed in 1774 and designed by William Chambers (1726–1796) for Sir Laurence Dundas. The Royal Bank of Scotland bought the building in 1825 and it is now their registered office.

The main banking hall was added by John Dick Peddie in 1857. It is almost 60ft (18m) square and its magnificent dome is pierced by 120 windows in the shape of six-pointed stars. The whole effect is simply breathtaking. Photography is allowed, but only of the upper section, as this is a working bank.

3 Exit Dundas House and pass to the right of the statue of John Hope, 4th Earl of Hopetoun (1765–1823), a distinguished army officer during the Napoleonic Wars and former governor of the bank. He is depicted in Roman guise and stands next to his horse, who is shorter than he is – allegedly the sculptor, Thomas Campbell, was not paid because of this error. Turn right onto St Andrew Square.

At the centre of the square is the Melville Monument (1823), a 121ft-high (37m) column topped by a statue of Henry Dundas (1724–1811), a key ally of William Pitt the Younger (1759–1806), for whom he was chief parliamentary fixer in Scotland. Such was his power that he was known as 'Harry the Ninth, uncrowned King of Scotland'. In 1805, however, he was impeached for corruption and, although restored to office, lost much of his influence.

4 Swing left over the crossing by Multrees Walk, keep ahead past the postbox and phone box and pause outside the second building from the end, which isn't numbered but is actually No. 22.

This was the birthplace of Dr Joseph Bell (1837–1911), who went on to become lecturer in medicine at the University of Edinburgh. In the days before X-rays he emphasized to his students the importance of close observation in making a diagnosis. To illustrate his point he would select a stranger and, by observing him, would deduce his occupation and recent activities. Arthur Conan Doyle studied under him at the university and later served as his clerk at

37

DISTANCE 2 miles (3.2km)

ALLOW 1.5–2 hours

START Duke of Wellington Statue on Princes Street opposite North Bridge

FINISH Princes Street at the bottom of Frederick Street

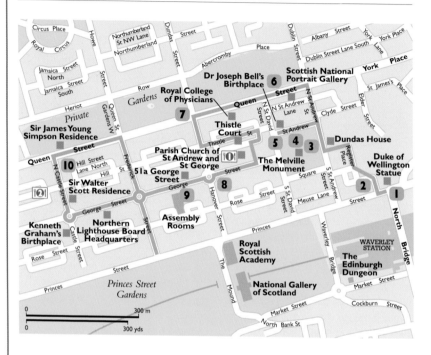

Edinburgh Royal Infirmary. Inspired by Bell's observational and deductive skills Conan Doyle created Sherlock Holmes, based on his old tutor.

5 Retrace your footsteps and go left down North St Andrew Street. Turn left along Queen Street and on the left is the Scottish National Portrait Gallery, a striking piece of neo-Gothic architecture built in the 1880s with money provided by John Ritchie Finlay, the owner of *The Scotsman* newspaper.

You can see everyone from Mary Queen of Scots and Bonnie Prince Charlie to Robbie Coltrane and Sir Alex Ferguson.
SCOTTISH NATIONAL PORTRAIT GALLERY;
www.nationalgalleries.org

6 Exit the gallery and go left along Queen Street, keeping ahead over North St David Street, and pause outside the Royal College of Physicians, at No. 9, designed in the late-Greek revival style by Thomas Hamilton in 1844.

The building's magnificent portico is adorned by three health-related statues depicting Hygeia flanked by Aesculapius and Hippocrates.

ROYAL COLLEGE OF PHYSICIANS;

www.rcpe.ac.uk

7 Continue, and go left into Hanover Street at the traffic lights. Turn first left into Thistle Street. Opposite Prospect House go right through the gates to pause outside Thistle Court. These are probably the oldest buildings in New Town and were put up around 1768. Exit the gates and go right, then next right onto Thistle Street South East Lane. Just after the car park on the left, go left through the covered passage, up the steps and ramp and right onto George Street. Immediately on the right is the Parish Church of St Andrew and St George, opened in 1784 and designed by Captain Andrew Frazer and Robert Kay.

James Craig's original plans for the New Town of Edinburgh included the building of two churches, St George's (for England) in Charlotte Square at the west end, and St Andrew's (for Scotland) in St Andrew's Square at the east end. Laurence Dundas, however, got in first, bought the land intended for St Andrew's, and built Dundas House on it. The church had to make do with this site. In 1964 the congregation of St George's Church in Charlotte Square was merged with that of St Andrew's to form the combined foundation of St Andrew's and St George's. The church is well worth a visit to admire the spectacular ceiling.

www.standrewsandstgeorges.org.uk

8 After your visit, exit the church and go right along George Street, keeping ahead over Hanover Street and pause outside No. 51. No. 51a was home for a time to Elizabeth (1851–1878) and Eugene Marie Chantrelle (1834–1878). Continue along George Street, go over Frederick Street and pause outside No. 81. By 1877 the Chantrelles had moved to No. 81a George Street.

Eugene was a French-born school teacher who married his pupil, Elizabeth Cullen Dyer, in 1868. The couple had four children. By the mid-1870s Chantrelle was drinking heavily, spending profusely, and slipping further into debt. He was also abusing his wife appallingly and even threatened to poison her. In October 1877 he took out an insurance policy for £1,000 on Elizabeth's life, which would pay out only in the event of accidental death, although he made careful enquiries as to exactly what would constitute accidental death. On New Year's Day 1878 Elizabeth was taken ill. A servant girl, who had been given the day off, returned the next morning to find her mistress unconscious. She was taken to the Royal Infirmary, where she died later that afternoon. Chantrelle claimed that she had been poisoned by a broken gas pipe in the main bedroom. But traces of opium were found in vomit stains on Elizabeth's night gown and Chantrelle was arrested and charged with poisoning his wife by administering opium in orange and lemonade. Following a four-day trial in May 1878, he was found guilty and hanged at Calton Jail on May 31st.

9 Cautiously cross over George Street. No. 84 is the headquarters of the Northern Lighthouse Board, with its flashing ornamental lighthouse over the door. Keep ahead to cross Castle Street and go left along it. On the wall of No. 30 is a plaque commemorating the birth here of Kenneth Graham, author of *Wind in the Willows*, on 8 March 1859. Backtrack, cross George Street via the zebra crossing, then go right, cross North Castle Street and turn left along it.

Pause outside No. 39, where Sir Walter Scott lived from 1802 to 1826 while at the peak of his success. When financial problems forced him to move he was devastated.

10 Keep ahead to the traffic lights, go right along Queen Street and pause outside No. 82, the home of

WHERE TO EAT

◎ **THE UNDERCROFT CAFÉ,**
St Andrew's and St George's Church, George Street;
Tel: No phone.
This café beneath St Andrew's and St George's Church offers a selection of sandwiches and snacks as well as warming soups. £

◎ **THE OXFORD BAR,**
8 Young Street;
Tel: 0131 539 7119.
A favoured watering hole with Scottish writers and artists. Among its regulars is mystery writer Ian Rankin, who has made it the local of his fictional sleuth Inspector Rebus. Several characters in his books are named after staff and regulars. £

obstetrician Sir James Young Simpson (1811–1870) from 1845 to 1870.

Here Simpson laboured to find a suitable alternative to ether as an anaesthetic, hazardously testing various volatile substances on himself. On 4 November 1847 he and his two assistants gathered in the dining room, inhaled chloroform for the first time and were 'rendered unconscious in a trice'. This discovery would help eliminate pain from both surgical operations and childbirth, gaining popularity after Queen Victoria gave birth under its influence. Take the next right into Frederick Street, cross George Street and keep ahead back into Princes Street.

41

Monuments, Follies and Pagan Fires

A lovely walk to the summit of Calton Hill, crowned by monuments that led to Edinburgh becoming known as 'the Athens of the north'.

Calton Hill is surely one of Edinburgh's most enduring images. Its monument-filled summit catches your gaze whenever you look up from many parts of the city. Photographers and artists strive to capture its many moods from as many different angles. Postcards carry its likeness all over the world. Those who take the trouble to endure the steep climb up its grassy slopes are rewarded with superlative views across the city, and find themselves wandering amidst many chapters of Edinburgh's history. Calton Hill is also the location for the annual spring fire festival of Beltane, on 30 April. The night's highlight is the procession of the May Queen to the four elemental points of the hill, followed by the death and rebirth of the Green Man and the lighting of a huge bonfire. This walk takes a slow spiralling route up the hill, beginning with a visit to a suitably eerie burial ground, before moving on through some of Edinburgh's grandest streets to begin a breathless ascent of the hill.

1 From the visitor centre go up the steps and turn right along **Princes Street**. Keep ahead over **North Bridge** and proceed along **Waterloo Place**. Pass the arches of the Regent Bridge, begun in 1816 and perhaps one of the most discreet bridges imaginable as it is only when you look through one of its central arches that you realize you are 50 or so feet (15m) above the road beneath. A little farther along, go right and through the gates of the **Old Calton Cemetery**. Climb the steps up to the soaring black obelisk.

The obelisk is the Political Martyrs Monument, designed by Thomas Hamilton in 1844 to commemorate Thomas Muir, Thomas Palmer, William Skirving, Maurice Margarot and Joseph Gerrald. These five brave men, advocates for political reform, were charged with sedition in 1793 and sentenced to transportation to Australia.

2 Backtrack a little and go left up the stone steps to the left of the iron railing, keeping ahead to the circular tomb of the philosopher **David Hume (1711–1776)**.

The tomb, designed by Robert Adam, is an eye-catching memorial to a genial man who was on friendly terms with just about everybody and who has been described as the most acute thinker in 18th-century Britain. The fact that he did not believe in either God or an afterlife led to rumours that he had sold his soul to the devil. Fearing that this might lead

to efforts to desecrate his grave, after his burial his friends mounted an eight-night vigil around his mausoleum with pistols and lanterns. Next to Hume's memorial stands Abraham Lincoln, which dates from 1893. This was the first statue of the president to be erected in Europe and commemorates Scottish-American soldiers killed in the American Civil War.

3 Leave the cemetery and go right along **Regent Road**, pausing to look through the gates at the Gothic and castellated former baronial-style **Governor's House**, about all that survives of the notorious old Calton Jail.

The jail dominated this section of Calton Hill from 1817 to 1925. Prisoners from all over Scotland were kept here prior to being tried at the Edinburgh High Court, and served their sentences here if convicted. Until 1864 executions used to take place on the jail roof watched by eager spectators from Calton Hill opposite. With the ending of public executions prisoners were put to death inside the prison, the first to die being wife-murderer Eugene Marie Chantrelle, whose story is covered in Walk 5. The prison was demolished in the 1930s and was replaced by St Andrew's House, the severe art deco civil service offices that stretch before you, which were opened in 1939.

4 Cross over the road via the central bollards and veer right. Just after the steps on the left, almost lost amidst the cloying greenery, is the memorial to

43

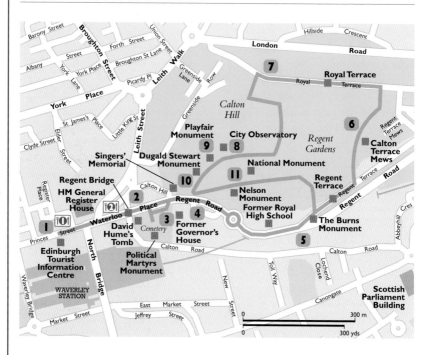

three famous Scottish singers – John Wilson (1800–1849), John Templeton (1802–1886) and David Kennedy (1825–1886), an ancestor of the violinist Nigel Kennedy. Continue as the road swings right, pause to take in the view of Salisbury Crags, with Arthur's Seat towering above them, then go over the driveway of Calton Hill Park and follow Regent Road as it swings left. A little further along on the left you pass the magnificent portico of the former Royal High School.

The school was designed by Thomas Hamilton between 1825 and 1829 and was based on the Temple of Theseus overlooking Athens. Continue and, just before Regent Terrace, look over the road at the Burns Monument, erected in 1830 and designed by Thomas Hamilton as a tribute to Scotland's greatest poet and songwriter, who died aged only 37. A statue of Burns once adorned the base but this has decamped to the National Portrait Gallery, leaving behind a memorial *sans* the remembered.

44

5 Veer left into Regent Terrace, an exceptionally handsome example of the city's New Town architecture. A fine line of Doric porches and trellis balconies stretches before you. Take the next left into Calton Terrace Lane and follow its cobblestones as they bear right, turning right into Calton Terrace Mews.

These attractive mews were once the abodes of the coach and carriage men who serviced the grand houses nearby. The properties still sport the ground-floor double doors behind which the carriages were kept, whilst the coachmen would have lived in the rooms above.

6 Backtrack and go right along Calton Terrace Lane. At the end turn left along Royal Terrace, the largest single continuous building in central Edinburgh.

Laid out between 1821 and 1860, its quarter mile (400m) length is lined by soaring houses with enormous ground-floor rooms. During the 19th century it was known as 'Whisky Row' because of the number of spirit merchants who bought the new properties.

7 Go left just before Greenside Parish Church, then sharp left again and ascend the steep stepped path, keeping the wall to your left. Just as it levels off, go right up the stone steps opposite the grey gate. Go right along the asphalt path and on the left is Parthenon look-alike, the National Monument.

These 12 magnificent Doric columns were conceived in 1816 as a memorial to Scotsmen who died in the Napoleonic Wars. Work began in 1822 to a design by Charles Robert Cockerell (1788–1863) and William Henry Playfair (1789–1857). The intention was to create a replica of the Parthenon in Athens, but unfortunately the costs proved enormous

and in 1830 the money simply ran out in. This led to the incomplete fragment of 12 columns that had been built being dubbed 'Edinburgh's shame' or 'Edinburgh's disgrace'.

8 Keep walking ahead along the asphalt path and go left in front of the City Observatory.

There are, in fact, two buildings. The Old Observatory, designed by James Craig, the architect behind the New Town, was begun in 1776 as a private venture intending to capitalize on the upper classes' fondness for astronomy. Unfortunately funding ran out and the building wasn't completed until 1792, by

which time there was insufficient money left for a telescope. The New Observatory was begun in 1818 by the Astronomical Institution and fulfilled the important function of providing an accurate time service for ships docked in the Port of Leith. It was designed by William Playfair and its important timepieces include the Politicians Clock – so called because it has two faces. In 1895 the smoke from railway trains and domestic fires led the Astronomer Royal for Scotland to decamp to Blackford Hill.

OLD OBSERVATORY;

www.astronomyedinburgh.org

9 Go right at the next corner, passing the Playfair Monument built by

William Playfair for his uncle, John Playfair (1748–1819), the first president of the Astronomical Institution and the main mover in the campaign to establish the City Observatory. Keep ahead along that path, and at the house at the end of this path follow the path to the left to the Dugald Stewart Monument.

Dugald Stewart (1753–1828) was greatly admired in his day but today is largely forgotten. He taught philosophy at Edinburgh University and was renowned for his learning, while his oratorical skills were such that one of his pupils commented that 'there was eloquence in his very spitting'. His monument, in the style of a Grecian temple, was designed by William Playfair and dates from 1831.

10 Go left in front of the monument, and when the path divides, take the right fork passing to the right of the cannon. Go right up the next path and pause by the railings to enjoy a superb view across Edinburgh. Backtrack, go right at the foot of the path and go up the next steps on the right to the left of the Nelson Monument.

This 100ft (33m) column was begun in 1807, two years after Nelson's death at the battle of Trafalgar. It resembles an upturned telescope and is surmounted by a large white time-ball that was added in 1852 and which still drops daily at 1pm. The base of the monument is divided into compartments that were intended to provide accommodation for disabled seamen. Unsurprisingly, disabled seamen

WHERE TO EAT

◎ THE GUILDFORD ARMS,
1 West Register Street;
Tel: 0131 556 4312.
Built in 1898, this real ale bar just off Princes Street boasts an opulent interior. Its chief glory is the magnificent Jacobean-style ceiling over the main bar. ££

◎ THE NEWS ROOM,
5–11 Leith Street;
Tel: 0131 557-5856.
A modern and lively venue that serves a variety of dishes including mussels and chips, burgers and sandwiches. £

were averse to having to struggle up the slopes of Calton Hill, so the idea was abandoned. If open, it is well worth the effort of climbing the 143 spiral stairs to the viewing platform.

11 Exit the Nelson Monument, go back down the steps then turn right and follow the path past the National Monument. When the path swings left, keep ahead across the grass to the stone cairn, built by keepers of the vigil for a Scottish parliament, which was kept at the foot of Calton Hill between 1992 and 1997, when Scotland voted to have its own Parliament. Carry on down the steps and turn right along the road. Once out of the gates, turn right past the phone box and walk back to Princes Street.

DECORATIONS AT THE BELTANE FESTIVAL

Long Ago Murder and Gruesome Goings-on

From the bustle of the Royal Mile this walk takes you on a voyage of discovery through the university and medical section of Edinburgh.

In the course of this wander you will weave through some tucked-away places that many people walk past on an almost daily basis without even realizing they exist. Having dealt with tales of bodysnatching, you move on to tales of a different kind when you see a place where author J K Rowling penned some of her early Harry Potter stories. Passing into the courtyard of the old university building you will learn of an infamous murder, before moving on to chortle at the escapades of the man who has been described as the world's 'best bad' poet. A highlight of the walk is the opportunity to explore the gruesome collections at the Surgeons Halls Museums, which are only open daily from 12 to 4, so take care to time the walk to ensure you that can visit them. Sir Walter Scott and Sir Arthur Conan Doyle are just two of the famous historical figures that you will encounter, whilst the chance of an esoteric meander through a mystical maze will certainly add a little variety to an eventful and fascinating stroll.

1 With your back to Tron Kirk, go right and right again along South Bridge, keeping ahead over Hunters Square to cross the pedestrian traffic light lights. Bear right and, at the next lights, go left into Infirmary Street.

Blackwell's bookshop on the right stands on the site where the first voluntary hospital in Scotland was opened on 6 August 1729. In 1836 it became the Royal Infirmary of Edinburgh. A little way along on the left you come to the former Lady Yester's Church, named for Margaret Ker, Lady Yester, who gave money for the building of a church in 1647. The current Gothic style building dates from 1804. Here the medical students could hear the bell signalling the start of an operation from their pews.

2 Continue along Infirmary Street and, as it bears left, keep ahead and go in through the gates. Ahead of you are the buildings of the former High School, now part of the University of Edinburgh. The High School was completed in 1777 and amongst those educated here was Sir Walter Scott. Following the school's departure for a site on Calton Hill in 1829, this building became a surgical hospital and later a fever hospital. It now houses the archaeology department of the University of Edinburgh. Pass through the arch to the right and keep ahead into Surgeons' Square.

The building in the far right corner was formerly Surgeons' Hall, built in 1697. Edinburgh surgeons conducted their business here until moving to their current headquarters in 1832. It was to this square that Burke and Hare used to bring the bodies of their victims for dissection at anatomy classes (see Walk 4).

3 Backtrack slightly and go left up the ramp to climb the steps into the car park. Bear right through the gates, the grand gateposts of which were designed by Robert Adam, and go right along Drummond Street. Keep ahead, passing the antiquated exterior of the former Rutherfords Bar on the right, built in 1834 and a regular haunt of both Robert Louis Stephenson and Arthur Conan

WHERE TO EAT

◉ PETERS YARD,
Middle Meadow Walk;
Tel: 0131 228 5876.
Scrumptious artisan bread straight out of the oven, gorgeous pastries, sandwiches and wholesome snacks and meals are offered at this restaurant in the new Quartermile development on the former site of Edinburgh Royal Infirmary. £

◉ THE BLIND POET,
2 West Nicholson Street;
Tel: 0131 667 0876.
This intimate Edinburgh hideaway has oodles of atmosphere and an almost world-weary ambience. A popular haunt with the university crowd, it serves a variety of reasonably priced pub food. Live music some nights. £

OPPOSITE: PLAYFAIR'S ROYAL COLLEGE OF SURGEONS

DISTANCE **2.5 miles (4km)**

ALLOW **2 hours**

START **Tron Kirk on the Royal Mile**

FINISH **Teviot Place**

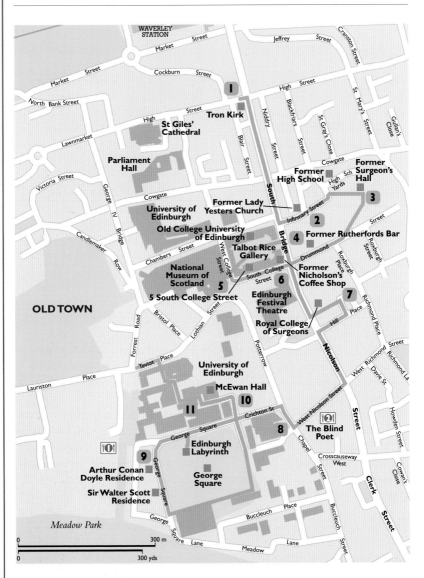

Doyle during their student days at the university. At the junction with Nicholson Street look over at the first floor of the Buffet King Chinese restaurant.

This was formerly Nicholson's Coffee Shop, where J K Rowling penned some of the early chapters of *Harry Potter and the Philosopher's Stone*.

4 Turn right along Nicholson Street, and cross it via the traffic lights outside Blackwells. Bear left, and turn right through the impressive portico of Edinburgh University's Old College, designed in 1789 by Robert Adam and completed by William Playfair between 1817 and 1840. The dome, which is considered one of Edinburgh's major landmarks, was added in 1884.

Old College is believed to stand on the site of Kirk o' Field, where one of the great unsolved mysteries of Scottish history occurred. In the early hours of the morning of the 10 February 1567, Edinburgh was rocked by a huge explosion. The source, it transpired, was the Old Provost Lodging of the Kirk o' Field, where Henry Stuart, Lord Darnley (1545–1567), the second husband of Mary, Queen of Scots, had been recuperating from illness. The partially clothed bodies of Darnley and his servant were found in a nearby orchard, but they had been strangled rather than killed in the explosion. Suspicion immediately fell on Mary and her most trusted nobleman, James Hepburn, Earl of Bothwell (1534–1578). He was subsequently tried and found not guilty of the crime, but the fact that Mary married him a mere three months after Darnley's death has added to speculation that they were responsible.

OLD COLLEGE;
www.ed.ac.uk/

5 Cross the courtyard and go up the first flight of steps to the war memorial. In front of it turn left then go right up the steps and through the passageway to the right of the Talbot Rice Gallery. Go left along West College Street, follow it as it bears left into South College Street and pause outside the black door of No. 5 on the right (next to the Captain's Arms pub). It was here that William McGonagall died on 29 September 1902.

William McGonagall (1852–1902) has been described as the world's best bad poet. A self-educated hand-loom weaver from Dundee, he discovered his talent for verse in 1877 and for the next 25 years delighted and appalled his audiences throughout Scotland and beyond. A group of students once bestowed on him the mock title Sir Topaz McGonagall, Knight of the order of the White Elephant, but mockery had little effect on him and he carried on regardless. On one occasion he walked all the way to Balmoral but was denied an audience with Queen Victoria, about whom he penned the following immortal lines:

'Long may she be spared to roam
Among the bonnie Highland floral,
And spend many a happy day
In the Palace of Balmoral.'

6 Go right along Nicholson Street, keeping straight on past the Festival Theatre. Cross Nicholson Street via the crossing, then bear left and turn right through the gates of the Royal College

of Surgeons of Edinburgh. Keep ahead along the path to go through the doors. Bear right and head for the desk in the right corner where you pay your admission. Once you have done so (or if the desk is unmanned) go through the door opposite to exit onto Hill Square. Three doors along on the left is the entrance to the Surgeons' Hall Museums.

Located within the historic 1832 Playfair Building and on the upper floors of an 18th-century tenement behind, the exhibitions displayed here chart the development of surgery from the 16th century to the modern day. The displays are fascinating, though sometimes macabre, and include such gems as a pocketbook made from the skin of the notorious murderer William Burke, of Burke and Hare infamy (see Walk 4).

7 Exit the museum, walk counterclockwise around Hill Square, go right along Hill Place and turn left onto Nicholson Street. At the lights go right along West Nicholson Street and cross to its left side. On the left is the Blind Poet pub.

The pub commemorates the poet Dr Thomas Blacklock (1721–1791), who lost his sight after contracting smallpox as a child. He and his wife lived in the upper rooms of West Nicholson House (now the Counting House and Pear Tree pub a few doors along). His greatest achievement was to persuade a despondent Robert Burns, who was on the verge of abandoning Scotland for the West Indies, to visit Edinburgh in 1786. Burns agreed and his visit proved an enormous success, bringing him fame and celebrity.

8 Turn right along Chapel Street, go over the crossing, and take the first left into Crichton Street. Keep ahead, then go left to go clockwise around George Square, Edinburgh's first major development outside the overcrowded Old Town, which was begun in 1766. Much of the square was decimated in the 1960s when the University of Edinburgh replaced most of its 18th-century buildings with the concrete monstrosities you see now.

Fortunately some of the older houses have survived, including the line on your left as you enter and those on the opposite side. Of this latter section, No. 25 was the childhood home of Sir Walter Scott from 1774 to 1797, and No. 23, a few doors farther along, was where Arthur Conan Doyle lived from 1876 to 1880 while studying medicine at Edinburgh University.

9 Continue walking clockwise around the Square.

Opposite the Hugh Robson Building, you might like to take a break by going into the gardens and exploring the Edinburgh Labyrinth, which offers the chance to 'relax or reflect while walking this ancient path'.

EDINBURGH LABYRINTH;

www.labyrinth.ed.ac.uk

10 Keep ahead, go left along Charles Street, turn left at the telephone box and go through the gates ahead.

To your right is the McEwan Hall, the University of Edinburgh's graduation hall, which was completed in 1897. Funded by the brewing magnate William McEwan, it was once described as resembling 'a magnificent petrified blancmange'.

11 Turn right in front of the bust of Archibald Campbell Tait, go left through the passageway and look around at the buildings of the Medical School, completed in 1886. Turn right and pass out through the gates, noting the plaques on the wall to former students, including Sir Arthur Conan Doyle. Bear left along Teviot Place and end your walk at the traffic lights. You can turn right here along Forrest Road and keep ahead along George IV Bridge and you will reach the Royal Mile.

Murder and Mystery in Morningside

Just a stone's throw from the bustle of the centre of Edinburgh you will find yourself walking quiet streets lined by some truly grand houses.

This is a walk filled with surprises. Firstly, it meanders through some of the most idyllic streets imaginable. Secondly, it has everything from notorious murders to intriguing history, and even encompasses the inspiration for Oscar Wilde's *The Picture of Dorian Gray*. You visit a childhood home of Sir Arthur Conan Doyle, the creator of Sherlock Holmes, and see the birthplace of the man on whom *The Last Emperor of China*, starring Peter O'Toole, was based. If all that is not enough to fascinate and intrigue then how about the school on which St Trinian's was based, which you will also pass. A large part of the walk is spent exploring Grange Cemetery so you will need to ensure that you allow enough time to arrive before it closes at 5pm. Otherwise, just take your time and absorb the ambience and admire the grand houses on the way.

1 Walk down the right side of Summerhall, go over Melville Terrace and ahead into Sciennes. Cross to its left side and turn second left into Sciennes House Place.

On the wall of No. 5 on the left is a plaque commemorating the meeting here of Robert Burns and a 15-year-old Sir Walter Scott in the winter of 1786–1787, the only time that Scotland's two most famous authors met.

2 Backtrack, go left into Sciennes Gardens then left again into Sciennes Hill Place to pause outside the last building on the left, No. 3, where Arthur Conan Doyle's family lived for a time in the 1860s. Backtrack into Sciennes, turn left into Sciennes Road, then first left into St Catherine's Place.

The Dominican convent of Catherine of Sienna was established here in 1517 but destroyed in 1559 during the Reformation. The name Sciennes is derived from the Convent's connections with Siena.

3 Turn right at the end of St Catherine's Place, go right along Grange Road and keep ahead into Beaufort Road. Go right into Palmerston Road. Pause outside No. 10, a little way along on the right.

It was here that Miss C Fraser Lee opened St Trinnean's School for girls in 1922. The 60 pupils were taught using the Dalton system of education, which

WHERE TO EAT

🍽 THE CANNY MAN'S,
37 Morningside Rd;
Tel: 0131 447 1484.
This pub-restaurant, with a warren of rooms crammed with antiques and curios, is an attraction in its own right. Booking is recommended for lunch and dinner. Tables are set outside in summer. ££

🍽 BODACIOUS,
219 Morningside Road;
Tel: 0131 466 3234.
This attractive little café offers freshly prepared light meals, tea, coffee, soft drinks and take-away snacks. Baked potatoes, soups and salads and plenty of organic healthy options. Yummy homemade cakes, too. £

🍽 TOAST,
146 Marchmont Road;
Tel: 0131 446 9873.
Hearty casseroles, warming soups as well as sandwiches and salads are on offer in this pleasant café, which uses locally sourced ingredients. £

advocated self-, as opposed to school-imposed, discipline, a system which led to its becoming known as the school 'where they do what they like'. The school was later immortalized as the fictional girls' boarding school St Trinian's in a series of cartoons by Ronald Searle, which later inspired the immensely popular series of comedy films.

57

DISTANCE 2.5 miles (5km)

ALLOW 2 hours

START The junction of Melville Drive and Summerhall (bus 42)

FINISH Old Parish Church, Morningside Road

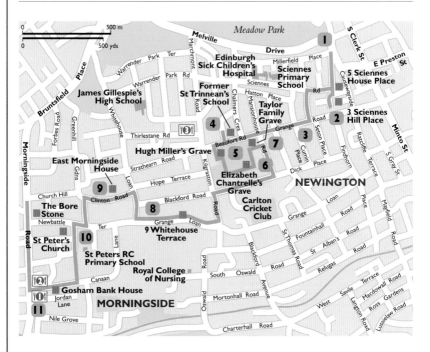

4 Go back and turn right along Beaufort Road, cross to its left side, and bear left. When the boundary wall ends, go left and left again through the gates of Grange Cemetery, where a little way along on the left, flanked by two Celtic crosses, is the tomb of Hugh Miller (1802–1856), an influential figure of 19th-century science and religion, whose life ended in tragedy.

Suffering from paranoia, on Christmas Eve 1856 Hugh Miller committed suicide by shooting himself in the heart in the bathroom of his home in Portobello.
www.hughmiller.org

5 A little way past the grave turn right and follow that path as it turns left just before a boundary wall. Keep ahead; just past the large tree on the right there is a distinctive grey cross to the Ursuline Nuns of St Margaret Convent. Opposite, across the path, is the large somewhat weathered gravestone of Joseph and Elizabeth Dyer.

Also buried here, but not remembered on the headstone, is their daughter Elizabeth Cullen Chantrelle (1851–1878) who was poisoned by her French born husband Eugene Marie Chantrelle (see Walk 5). On the day of her funeral her murderous spouse feigned a grief-stricken passionate outburst and attempted to throw himself onto the grave with her coffin.

6 Keep ahead, ignoring the first left turn, and follow the path as it turns left. On the left, just after the domed monument of James Thomas, is the grave of former foreign secretary Robin Cook (1946–2005). Continue and, just after a path on the left, go down the steps where, immediately after the grave of John Grant Roos, go right. Some way along on the left is one of the cemetery's more striking graves, that of James Smith (1824–1887), and, after the tree, go right along the grass path to cross over the gravel path and walk over to the boundary wall.

Five graves along from the fence to your left is the memorial stone to Michael Taylor (died 18 May 1867), his wife Jane (died 25 February 1865) and their 'beloved daughter' Mary Jane Pritchard (died 18 March 1865, aged 38 years.) Following Mary Jane's death exactly three weeks after that of her mother, her husband Dr Edward William Pritchard was arrested and charged with poisoning her. Traces of antimony were found in her liver, and since her mother Jane had died suffering similar symptoms, her body was exhumed and traces of antimony were found in it also. Dr Pritchard was duly tried at Edinburgh's High Court, found guilty of murder and hanged in Glasgow on 28 July 1865.

7 Go back and turn right along the red gravel path to exit the cemetery through the gates. Turn right (note the old drinking fountain on the wall dated 1889), right again past the waist-high

fence and squeeze through the very narrow passage, locally known as 'Lovers Loan,' at the end of the first section of which go right along Dick Place. At the end of Dick Place turn left along Kilgraston Road and right into Whitehorse Terrace. Pause outside No. 9.

This was the home of André Sebastian Raffalovich (1864–1934), a wealthy Russian émigré Jew who converted to Catholicism and funded the building of nearby St Peter's Church, visited later in the walk, for his friend Canon John Gray.

8 Keep going along Whitehouse Terrace, a long walk made pleasant by the obvious affluence of houses that hide behind the high walls, and go right into Whitehouse Loan. Cross to its left side and take the first left into Clinton Road. Pause on the right by the gateposts of No. 5, East Morningside House.

An inscription remembers the author Susanne Ferrier (1782–1854), often referred to as the Scottish Jane Austen, who was born here.

9 Continue, taking time to admire the large villas set back behind the high walls. Go left along Pitsligo Road, at the foot of which go right along Newbattle Terrace, then first left into Falcon Gardens. On the right is St Peter's Church, built in two stages between 1906 and 1929. Its first priest was Father John Gray.

Born in poverty in Woolwich, London, Gray became involved with Oscar Wilde, whom he met in the summer of 1889. When Wilde turned his affections to Lord Alfred Douglas, Gray became suicidal and was rescued by Andre Raffalovich, with whom he collaborated on several plays. He converted to Catholicism, became a priest in 1901, and was a curate at St. Patrick's Canongate before moving to St Peter's.

ST PETER'S CHURCH;

www.stpetersrcchurchedinburgh.org.uk/

10 Keep to the left side of Falcon Gardens, descend the steps beyond the fence and follow the path to the right of St Peter's School. When it ends, go over the zebra crossing and bear right along Canaan Lane. Some way along on the left you come to two single-storey cottages, Nos. 22 and 20. Look through the gap between the cottages and you can see Gosham Bank House, a fine, tucked-away villa that was the birthplace of Reginald Johnson.

Johnson grew up in the city and studied at Edinburgh University, later to become tutor to the last emperor of China prior to the republican revolution of 1912. Another view of the house can be had by going through the arch after No. 18 and looking left above the garages.

11 At the end of Canaan Lane go right along Morningside Road, crossing over Newbattle Terrace, till you arrive at the church, now part of Napier University. A little way along on its wall is the Bore Stone, where the Royal Standard was last pitched for the muster of the Scottish army before the Battle of Flodden in 1513. This is where the walk ends. Cross Morningside Road and bear left to come to a bus stop for a bus back to the city centre.

61

OPPOSITE: ST PETER'S CHURCH; ABOVE: FLODDEN STONE

DEAN VILLAGE

Edinburgh's Secret Village

Stroll through a picturesque village and along a rural footpath to reach a peaceful cemetery where the famous from bygone Edinburgh lie buried.

Originally known as the Village of the Water of Leith, Dean Village evolved around a milling community. Milling was carried out from at least the 12th century and numerous mills were operated here by the town of Edinburgh and by the Incorporation of Baxters (Bakers). Its industrial heyday is now long gone, but the village is a picturesque architectural gem that nestles in its tranquil valley beneath the mighty span of Thomas Telford's impressive Dean Bridge, on which your walk begins. From here you begin the deep descent to explore a sequence of fascinating buildings that date from many different ages. You then enjoy an idyllic stroll along one of the most attractive reaches of the Water of Leith Walkway to emerge at Dean Gallery, where you can enjoy its modern art collection. From here you stroll through Dean Cemetery to visit the graves of the real-life inspiration for Sherlock Holmes and one of Edinburgh's tragic heroes. Passing through another section of Dean Village you arrive at a graceful Roman Temple that stands over a famed medicinal well. Parts of the route can be muddy so sensible footwear is encouraged.

1 Cross to the centre of the bridge and look down at the Water of Leith tumbling 108ft (33m) beneath you.

The bridge was designed by Thomas Telford and opened in 1832, allowing much better communications and access from the west and north into Edinburgh. When the bridge opened, its low parapet made it a popular spot for suicides. As a result it acquired the nickname 'Bridge of Sighs', and, in an attempt to discourage this unforeseen usage, the parapet was eventually raised.

2 Backtrack off the bridge to see the strange building on the right.

This building was a tavern in the 17th century before being converted into a baronial house in the 1890s. It is actually bigger than it looks because, although only two storeys are visible at bridge level, another three cling precariously to the sides of the precipice beneath.

3 Turn right and begin the steep descent of Bell's Brae, which was the main road from the north and west into the city before Dean Bridge was built. Observe the tall yellow building on the left, which was Baxters' Tolbooth.

The tolbooth was built in 1675 and was the headquarters of the Incorporation of Baxters (Bakers) and was also used as their granary; now been converted into flats. Above the blocked doorway note the lintel that bears the motto *'God bless the Baxters of Edinbrugh who built this*

hous 1675'. The carving above it has the Baxters' crossed peels or shovels, which were used to remove hot bread from the oven. It also depicts three cakes and a pie along with the inscription *'God's Providenc is our inheritenc'*.

4 Keep ahead into Hawthornbank Lane, passing the Hawthorn Buildings (1895) with their curious half-timbered upper stories, which date from 1895. Descend the steep cobblestone ramp. Pause to look over the river at one of the best views of the extraordinary Well Court.

This was designed by Sidney Mitchell in 1886 for John Ritchie Findlay, proprietor of *The Scotsman*, who wanted to provide decent housing for working class tenants, but also wanted to treat himself to something unusual to look at from his house in the western New Town.

65

DISTANCE **2 miles (3.2km)**

ALLOW **1.75 hours**

START **Dean Bridge**

FINISH **North West Circus Place**

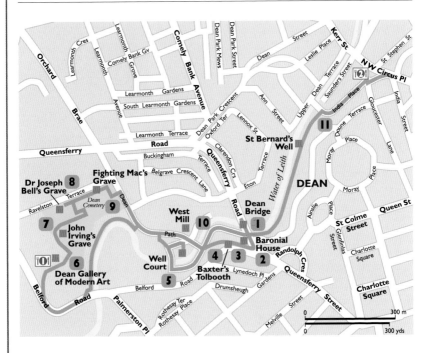

5 Go right over the small footbridge into Damside and turn right, then right again through the arch into the courtyard of Well Court to admire it from within. Backtrack through the arch and go left along Damside, turning right onto Upper Damside and, just past the iron gate of the Scottish Power Electricity enclosure, squeeze through Convening Court to the right, go up the steps to turn left and ascend Dean Path. Once past the block of yellow flats you come to a long wall on the left. Go left

through its gate and descend the steps to the Water of Leith Walkway. Turn right and keep ahead along this lovely, almost rural path up to the bridge then go right and up the steps, keeping ahead onto Belford Road to turn right through the gate into the grounds of the Dean Gallery of Modern Art.

This houses a world-class collection of Dada and Surrealism and works by the Scottish sculptor Eduardo Paolozzi (b1924). The building was formerly the

Dean Orphan Hospital built in 1833 and designed by Thomas Hamilton.

DEAN GALLERY OF MODERN ART;

www.nationalgalleries.org

6 Go left off the gallery steps, left again just before the sign board, and as the path sweeps left, go right and follow the chipped bark path that hugs the wall, turning right through the gate of Dean Cemetery.

Go left to reach the Celtic cross to the right of the bushes and read the moving story of John Irving (1815–1848/49) of HMS Terror, a member of Sir John Franklin's ill-fated expedition to find the North West Passage. He died on the frozen wastes of King William's Land, where he was initially buried. Some 33 years later his grave was found and his remains brought back to Edinburgh and laid to rest at Dean Cemetery in 1881.

7 Follow the path to the left of his monument as it curves right, then some way along, turn left between the two trees to go through the gap in the wall. Turn left, then right, keep ahead past the pink granite obelisk, and go left at the grave of John Harrison by the boundary wall.

Two graves along on the right is the grave of Dr Joseph Bell, on whom Sir Arthur Conan Doyle based his immortal sleuth Sherlock Holmes.

8 Go back past the grave of John Harrison, keep ahead along the path and, six graves after the second path to the right, you reach the grave of Major General Sir Hector Archibald MacDonald (1853–1903), a brilliant soldier and popular army commander who rose from very humble beginnings to achieve high office in the British army.

In 1902 'Fighting Mac', as he was affectionately known by his men, was appointed commander of the troops in Ceylon. Here accusations that he was homosexual began to circulate and were picked up by the press. Macdonald set off for London to answer the charges via the Hotel Regina in Paris. Reading in the newspaper of the scandal, he went back to his room and shot himself in the head with his revolver. His body was brought back to Edinburgh and buried amidst great secrecy in the early hours of the morning. By a strange coincidence it was announced that Colonel August von Mackensen of the Prussian Army had died in a Berlin military hospital on the same day as MacDonald's suicide, although some months later it was announced that von Mackensen was still alive, rising to rank of field marshal. The fact that he bore an uncanny resemblance to MacDonald led to rumours that the Paris suicide had been rigged and that he had in fact gone over to the Germans and taken the place of von Mackensen.

9 Continue ahead and go right when you arrive at the boundary wall. Keep straight on and exit the cemetery through the gates on the left. Turn right and descend Dean Path, pausing some way down on the left by West Mill.

There has been a mill on the site since the 15th century, although the present building dates from 1805, built by the Incorporation of Baxters and converted to flats in 1973.

10 Keep ahead over the bridge and turn left along Miller Row. Just after the cobbles end and the asphalt bends right, go left through the gap in the wall, where there is an information board about Lindsay's Mill, from which just three millstones remain. Go back through the gap in the wall, go left and gaze up at the graceful span of Dean Bridge high above you. Keep ahead past the curiously ornate yet down-at-heel-looking little building that was built in 1912 as a squash court. Pass under the bridge into The Dene, passing the windowless structure of St George's Well, inscribed with the date 1810.

WHERE TO EAT

🍽️ **DEAN GALLERY OF MODERN ART CAFÉ,**
73 Belford Road;
No phone.
This pleasant eatery in the art gallery makes for a good refreshment stop before beginning your dalliance with the dead in Dean Cemetery. The café offers coffee, sandwiches, soups of the day and light meals. £

🍽️ **SONGKRAN II,**
8 Gloucester Street;
Tel: 0131 225 4804.
Located in the house where landscape painter David Roberts was born, this snug Thai restaurant is situated at the end of the walk, making for a pleasant location in which to wind down. ££

A little farther along you arrive at the far more ornate, St Bernard's Well.

The present Roman temple was added by Lord Gardenstone in 1789. It is an elegant structure in the form of a Doric rotunda surmounted by a lead dome, under which stands a marble statue of Hygeia, goddess of health.

11 Continue and, at St Bernard's Bridge, go up the steps, turn right at the top and turn left along India Place at the end of which go right onto North West Circus Place. Cross over to the bus stop for a bus back to the city centre.

Greyfriars Kirkyard, Edinburgh's Necropolis

Greyfriars Kirkyard has been called Edinburgh's Westminster Abbey because of the number of famous former citizens who lie buried here.

This walk starts at the statue of Greyfriars Bobby, whose loyalty to his dead master was a true Victorian tear-jerker. You then enter the gates of the cemetery and begin your wander among the dead of Edinburgh. Although the route is mapped out for you, keep your eyes peeled for some astonishing ornamental graves, not to mention eerie skulls and tombstones. One of the surprising things about Greyfriars Kirkyard is just how quiet it is. Surrounded by the busy streets of Edinburgh the roar of the traffic hardly penetrates its sturdy walls. This is also a hugely historical place, for it was at Greyfriars Kirk that the National Covenant was signed in 1638 in protest at Charles I's attempts to bring the separate churches of England and Scotland together by the introduction of a new *Book of Canons* and a modified form of the Book of Common Prayer into Scotland. This in turn gave its name to the Covenanters, who sided with Parliament during the Civil War and were thus persecuted after Charles II regained the throne in 1660. All in all this is a fascinating, if slightly macabre stroll.

Start the walk by reading the plaque that remembers Bobby's affectionate fidelity (see No. 2 below). Go through the gates to the left of Bobby's Bar, keep ahead along the uneven cobblestones, pass through the next gates beneath the old lantern and enter Greyfriars Kirkyard.

Ahead of you is Greyfriars Kirk, built in 1629 and restored in 1938, which stands on the site of a 15th-century Franciscan Friary. It was inside the Kirk that the National Covenant was signed in 1638. There is a historical exhibition inside.

GREYFRIARS KIRK;

www.greyfriarskirk.com

2 Directly ahead of you, just before the Kirk, is the memorial stone to Greyfriars Bobby, the world's most famous Skye terrier, who died on 14 January 1872 aged 16 years. When his master, John Gray (1813–58), died, the faithful Bobby accompanied the funeral procession and then kept a 14-year vigil at the graveside. Go right in front of the grave and pass through two black bollards to the right of the information board. Keep ahead along the path, noting the skulls, cross bones, hourglasses and other macabre *memento mori* carved onto the tombs that line your way.

A little way along on the left, pink cobblestones surround the gravestone of John Gray 'Old Jock', the master of Greyfriars Bobby.

3 Keep ahead along the gravel path and, at its end, just before the single

black bollard, go right and pause in front of the very weathered Martyrs Monument. This monument commemorates the 100 or so Covenanters who lie buried in a trench to the west of the monument. Walk past the black bollard, go right onto the cobbled path, turn left through the two black bollards to follow the gravel path.

Just past the tree on your left is the memorial stone to Duncan Ban Macintyre (1724–1812), who, despite the fact he never learned to read, was one of the most prominent Gaelic Poets. This intricately carved tomb was erected by 'a few admirers of his genius'.

4 Walk back towards the path, passing the small flat stone on the ground that commemorates James Craig (1744–95), the architect of the New Town. Walk directly ahead and pause to look in through the gate at the blackened cloaked figure that seems to

OPPOSITE: GREYFRIARS KIRKYARD; ABOVE: GREYFRAIRS BOBBY

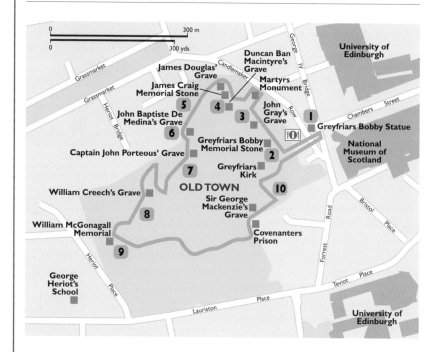

Duncan Ban Macintyre's Grave
James Douglas' Grave
James Craig Memorial Stone
Martyrs Monument
University of Edinburgh
John Baptiste De Medina's Grave
John Gray's Grave
Chambers Street
Greyfriars Bobby Statue
Captain John Porteous' Grave
Greyfriars Bobby Memorial Stone
National Museum of Scotland
Greyfriars Kirk
William Creech's Grave
OLD TOWN
Sir George Mackenzie's Grave
William McGonagall Memorial
Covenanters Prison
George Heriot's School
Lauriston Place
University of Edinburgh

hover eerily, a sinister looking skull leering at you from its right side. Go left along the path as it bears left and pause by the solitary stump of stone on the ground with the initials JEM.

This is the grave of James Douglas, 4th Earl of Morton (1516–81), Regent of Scotland during the minority of James VI and the leader of the group that assassinated David Rizzio (1533–66), Mary, Queen of Scots' faithful secretary at Holyrood Palace. He was later condemned to death for complicity in the murder of Lord Darnley (Mary's second husband) and on 2 June 1581 was beheaded by the 'Maiden', an early form of guillotine that he himself had introduced into Scotland from Halifax, having been 'impressed by its clean work'.

5 Keep ahead to the wall and pause before the large tomb with the twisted columns. This tomb is that of Thomas Bannatyn (1570–1635). It shows an angelic figure stamping on a skeleton's

72

ribcage whilst Old Father Time leans on an hourglass with his scythe above his head. Backtrack slightly and go right onto the grass to the tomb immediately to the left of Sir Thomas Hope, advocate to Charles I, who died in 1646.

Two headless figures stand on either side of this curious memorial, with two hands across joined across a leering skull. A fat baby surmounts the tomb, leaning on a skull in front of a depiction of Holyrood Palace. Continue up the grass and, on the right, just before the steps on the right, is another curious tomb, of the Spanish portrait painter John Baptiste De Medina (1659–1710) adorned with skulls and crossbones and a grille through which you can peer into its darker interior.

6 Go up the steps and, just as the path starts to bend right, on the right is the simple slab grave of John Porteous, Captain of the Edinburgh City Guard, who was murdered by an angry mob on 7 September 1736. For more on this story see Walk 4.

7 Continue along the path and go right to pass through the arch of the Flodden Wall. Turn right along the first path, go left at its end, then turn left up the grass slope onto the path where, by the first tree on the left, you will find the grave of William Creech (1745–1815).

Creech was bookseller, publisher and Lord Provost. He also managed to incur the wrath of the poet Robert Burns by withholding some of the money for his poems. Incensed, Burns responded with a literary attack:

*'A little pert, tart, tripping wight
And still his precious self his dear delight;
Who loves his own smart shadow in the streets
Better than e'er the fairest she he meets.'*

8 Continue up the path and pause by the gates on the right to look ahead into the grounds of George Heriot's School. To the left of the gates is the plaque to Walter Geikie (1795–1837), 'deaf artist of renown', inscribed with

the lines, 'Come join wi' me, folk of Auld Reekie. To weave a wreath for glorious Geikie.' To his left is a memorial to William McGonagall (1825–1902).

McGonagall is renowned as the world's best bad poet, whose poems still sell to this day and whose memorial here contains his immortal lines, 'I am your Gracious Majesty ever faithful to Thee. William McGonagall The Poor Poet That lives in Dundee.'

9 Go back through the arch of the Flodden Wall. Here a very small stone on the ground, its inscription almost illegible, commemorates Walter Scott Esq the father of Sir Walter Scott. Go right along the black gravel path to the padlocked gate, where a plaque on the wall to the left gives the history of the Covenanters Prison, so called because it was long believed that 1,200 captured Covenanters were held here following their defeat in 1679. Go left along the path in front of the gates and a little farther along on the right is the domed canopied tomb of Sir George Mackenzie (1636–91).

Mackenzie was the advocate responsible for the successful prosecution of many Covenanters, hence his nickname, 'Bluidy Mackenzie'. Regarded as a 'species of ogre' by the people of Edinburgh, his tomb was long believed to be haunted and it used to be customary for children to shout through the keyhole, 'Bluidy Mackenzie, come out if ye daur. Lift the snek and draw the bar'. They would

WHERE TO EAT

🍽 BOBBY'S BAR,
34 Candlemaker Row;
Tel: 0131 225 8328.
Portraits of the loyal pooch adorn the walls along with stills form the Walt Disney film that carried the name of Greyfriars Bobby across America. It is conveniently situated by the gates of Greyfriars Kirkyard. £

then run off lest Mackenzie obliged! More recently, there have been hundreds of reported poltergeist attacks on those visiting the tomb on the city's ghost walks. Visitors have reportedly been touched, pulled, grabbed and even slapped.

10 Continue along the path. When you reach the tree on the left go left, descend the grass slope to two iron security cages that cover a grave. As the city's major burial ground, Greyfriars was particularly vulnerable to the nocturnal activities of the bodysnatchers and these mortsafes were intended to provide some protection for the bodies of the newly dead. Go right along the path and follow it as it bears left. Pause by the church window.

Here a carved stone to its right shows a prancing skeleton with prominent ribcage, swinging a scythe and holding the *Book of Destiny* – a grim relic on which to end your tour as you go out through the gates opposite and rejoin the world of the living.

OPPOSITE: MEMORIAL STONE IN GREYFRIARS KIRKYARD

EDINBURGH CASTLE WITH ST CUTHBERT'S CHURCH IN THE FOREGROUND

Bodysnatchers, Spectres and Civil War

Beginning with a visit to one of Edinburgh's most atmospheric burial grounds, this is a walk of many contrasts.

Tales of bodysnatching get this stroll off to a sinister start as you stand in what can be a truly creepy kirk yard. Having paid your respects at the graves of the architect who designed the Scott Monument and of celebrated opium eater Thomas De Quincey, you confront modern Edinburgh head on as you negotiate the traffic and the crowds on the busy Lothian Road. Pausing to search for the ghost of a famous Victorian actress, the walk continues on to the head of the Union Canal, on which the murderers Burk and Hare laboured as navvies. Following its towpath you find yourself (at the time of writing) surrounded by decaying industrial premises, which, nonetheless, have a creepily sinister ambience about them. The next section meanders through one of Edinburgh's more sought after residential districts, Merchiston, where writers such as J K Rowling and Ian Rankin live. Entering the campus of Napier University, you might wonder what is mysterious or historic about the gleaming modern glass and steel structures that surround you but, read on, there is a fittingly dramatic finale to your stroll.

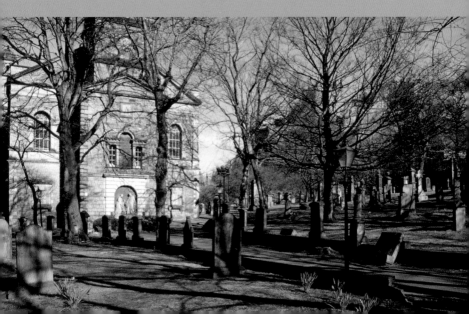

1 Go through the gates, down the steps and descend the path through the gateposts of St Cuthbert's Kirk.

Reputedly there has been a place of worship on this site since the 7th century, when St Cuthbert (AD634–687) built a tiny hut by the side of the stream that later became the Nor Loch. The current church dates from 1894, although its steeple was built in 1789. It is a massive structure that towers over you and a late 19th-century description of it as looking like a 'huge stone box…that resembles a packing-case' isn't far off the mark.

ST CUTHBERT'S KIRK;
www.st-cuthberts.net

2 Turn right down the two steps through the smaller posts and walk between the graves to go left through the gap in the wall just after the second tree.

The iron tomb that you pass on the right is worth a brief glance, looking as it does more like an oven than a grave!

3 Keep ahead over the grass, go right along the asphalt path and proceed counter-clockwise round the church's exterior to its main door. Veer right along the path opposite the entrance, go past the black barrier and pass the large building to your right. When the path bends right, go left through the gap in the railing, left again, passing the tomb of William Oliphant, and, once inside the grass enclosure, walk diagonally right to the impressive large tombstone located between the two trees.

WHERE TO EAT

[1] ZUCCA AT THE LYCEUM,
15–17 Grindlay Street;
Tel: 0131 221 9323.
An Italian-style café at the Royal Lyceum Theatre that serves up meat and fish dishes as well as spaghetti and salads. £££

[2] CARGO EDINBURGH QUAY,
129 Fountainbridge, Tollcross;
Tel: 0131 659 7880.
A gleaming new bar designed to appeal to a hip clientele, Cargo offers an extensive, imaginative menu. Dishes include Stornoway black pudding fritters with red onion marmalade and smoked chicken, roast red pepper and petit pois macaroni with garlic cream. The portions are generous. ££

This is the grave of George Meikle Kemp (1795–1844) the brilliant architect of the Scott Monument. The son of a Peebleshire shepherd, Kemp trained as a joiner and taught himself architecture. Four years after Scott's death in 1832 his admirers decided to honour his memory with a suitably Gothic monument and a competition to find a designer was announced. There were 55 entrants, and 45-year-old Kemp, fearing that his lack of architectural qualifications would disqualify him, entered under the pseudonym John Morvo, the name of the medieval architect of Melrose Abbey. His design was chosen from a

DISTANCE **2.5 miles (4km)**

ALLOW **2 hours**

START **St Cuthbert's on Princes Street, opposite South Charlotte Street**

FINISH **Holy Corner on Morningside Road**

shortlist of three. Sadly, he never lived to see his masterpiece completed as he was drowned in the Union Canal in March 1844. It was originally mooted that his remains would be deposited in a vault under the Scott Monument, but this proved impractical and he was buried here in St Cuthbert's Kirkyard, his soaring masterpiece visible through the trees beyond his grave.

4 Backtrack past the barrier and go left in front of the main church door. Just after the line of four graves, turn left up the steps into the eeriest section of the walk. Follow the path as it swings right, passing to your left a line of seemingly derelict vaults, their toppled masonry, crumbling walls, and dark interiors sufficient to elicit cold shivers even in bright sunshine. You then pass a line of waist-high tombstones, from which leering skulls gaze solemnly up at you. Follow the path as it bears left, and pause at the eighth wall grave on the left (the one with the semi-circular top), that of Thomas De Quincey (1785–1859).

De Quincey was author of *Confessions of an English Opium Eater.*

5 Turn your back on De Quincey's grave and head for the round, battlemented tower that you can see

over the top of the draped urn to your right. This is St Cuthbert's Watchtower, built in 1827 to enable the church to protect the bodies of the newly dead from the attentions of bodysnatchers.

The church's location outside the protection of the Old Town made its burial ground a magnet for the resurrectionists. The problem of corpse stealing was such that in 1738 the walls of the churchyard were raised to 8ft (2.5m) to make nocturnal entry hard, and getting a freshly dug up body out of the burial ground even harder. Two years later, the Kirk Session appointed an officer to keep records of the dead. However, kirk officers could still be bribed and when, in 1742, several bodies were illicitly removed, one of the beadles was suspected of complicity in the crime and an angry mob reacted by burning his house down. The problem persisted, and in 1803 a watchman was appointed to guard the graveyard by night. The watch house was built in 1827, by which time moves were afoot to end the problem with a change to the law. In 1832 the Anatomy Act allowed people to leave their bodies to medical science as well as entitling physicians, students and surgeons access to unclaimed bodies. Thus the need to steal corpses came to an end and bodysnatching became a thing of the past.

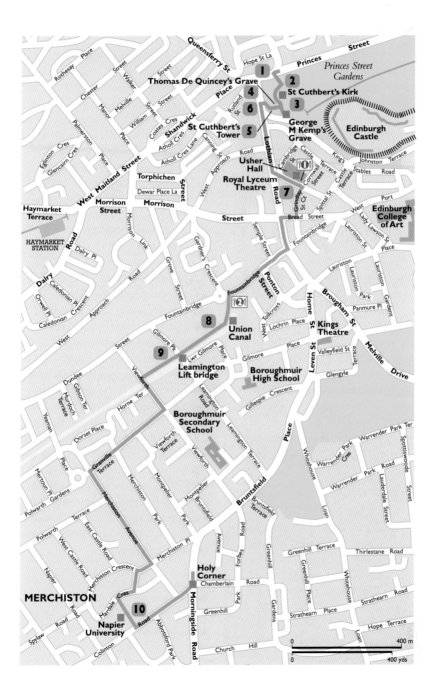

6 Ascend the steps to the right of the watchtower, exit the gates and go left along Lothian Road. Forge ahead over King's Stables Road and Castle Terrace, your way lined by towering structures of gleaming modernity, which give way as you enter Festival Square to the more pleasing aspect of the Usher Hall, Edinburgh's premier concert hall built in 1914 with a bequest of £100,000 from the beer magnate Andrew Usher. Go left along Grindlay Street and pause a little way along on the left outside the Royal Lyceum Theatre.

The theatre opened in 1883 with a two-week run of *Much Ado About Nothing* performed by Henry Irving and the London Lyceum Company. This marked the first appearance in Edinburgh of the great actress Ellen Terry (1847–1928). Several ghosts are known to roam the theatre's sumptuous interior, including a blue lady, which some think may actually be the shade of Ellen Terry herself. She is mostly seen in the gallery, the level above the Upper Circle, which has been closed to the public since 1966. She either walks past astonished witnesses and then disappears, or simply stands looking down at the stage, waves to cast members and melts away into thin air. Apparently, there was once a chalk statue of Ellen Terry in the theatre's foyer, but during World War II, when chalk was in demand, the statue was broken up and only the head survived.

ROYAL LYCEUM THEATRE;

www.lyceum.org.uk

7 Just after the Lyceum Theatre, steel into the gloom-laden Grindlay Street Court on the right. The initial chilling ambience that you encounter quickly gives way to ugly modern buildings. So hurry through it, go right along Bread Street, turn left at the traffic lights and rejoin Lothian Road. At East Fountain Bridge Road, pause to look at the colourful mosaic above the door of Lloyds TSB bank with its curtailed Shakespearean quote, 'Thrift is blessing'. Go right over Lothian Road by the traffic lights, proceed along the left side of Fountainbridge, and keep ahead over Thornybauk and Ponton Street. Just after Cargo, go left along the cobbled walkway to the Union Canal.

The canal was built between 1818 and 1822 to transport coal to Edinburgh. Thousands of Irish navvies laboured to dig out and construct the canal that runs from Edinburgh to Falkirk, a total distance of 31 miles (50km), among

them William Burke and William Hare, the infamous West Port murderers (see Walk 4).

8 Head along the right towpath, which has the air of neglect about it. Keep ahead past the Leamington Lift Bridge.

The bridge was built in 1896 and moved to its current location in the 1920s. It was restored in 2002 and you may have the good fortune to watch it lifting to allow canal boats to pass beneath.

9 At the next bridge, go up the steps, turn left along Viewforth, right along Gilmore Place into Granville Terrace, then left into Merchiston Avenue. Admire the large houses that line your way. Having traversed its entire length, go right along Merchiston Crescent. Keep to its left side to turn right into Mardale Crescent, cross immediately to the left side and, just after the two trees, go left through the concrete posts to bear right, then swing left through the buildings of Napier University.

Here a true surprise awaits you for, nestling at the heart of the modern buildings, stands what is surely Edinburgh's most hidden castle, Merchiston Castle or Tower, built around 1454 by Alexander Napier. Famous as the birthplace of John Napier (1550–1617), mathematician and the inventor of logarithms, the castle came under bombardment in 1572 during the strife that followed the abdication of Mary Queen of Scots in favour of her son James VI. A 26lb (12kg) cannon ball found embedded in the tower during restoration in the 1960s probably dates from this conflict.

10 Continue ahead, go left along Colinton Road and pause at the junction, which is straddled by four churches on each corner so became known in Victorian times as 'Holy Corner', the name by which it is still known locally today. Turn left and walk to the bus stop. From here you can take a bus back to the city centre.

83

Hermits, Stargazers and a Sylvan Hideaway

This lovely walk through one of Edinburgh's most idyllic landscapes encompasses both intriguing history and some fantastic views.

The terrain on this walk was shaped long ago by volcanic activity and glaciers. Blackford Hill is an Edinburgh landmark that, although not particularly high, certainly provides good exercise as you trudge up its slopes. But those breathless steps prove worth it, for once on the summit you will be rewarded with some of the most stunning views that Edinburgh has to offer. From this lofty height you will then descend into a delightful wooded glen through which babbles a sparkling burn. Suddenly the noise of modern Edinburgh has all but disappeared to be replaced by the twittering of birds and the rustling of leaves. Meandering along these woodland paths, it is hard to believe that a busy capital city is but a stone's throw away, and the overall ambience is one of pure magic. Set amidst this sylvan landscape you will discover one of Edinburgh's most curious houses, the battlemented and turreted Hermitage House, dating from 1785 and home to an intriguing exhibition on the history and features of this lovely area.

Ascend the right side of Blackford Avenue and go right along Observatory Road. Pass through the red sandstone arch, which was built in 1887 to commemorate the life and work of Lord Provost Sir George Harrison. Once through the arch, climb steeply up the pleasant house-lined street. The stunning views across the Edinburgh skyline to your right provide ample excuse for frequent pauses to catch your breath. Turn right after No. 22, take the left uphill path then go right along the grass path, passing on the left the buildings of the Royal Observatory.

Edinburgh's original Royal Observatory was on Calton Hill. But by 1888, a combination of inadequate buildings, outdated instruments and light pollution from the surrounding city had rendered it all but obsolete and the possibility of handing its buildings over to the University of Edinburgh was seriously considered. However, the Earl of Crawford gifted the contents of his well-equipped astronomy and library in Aberdeenshire to the nation, and the government agreed to build a new complex on Blackford Hill to accommodate it. The current complex was built in 1892 and now houses the UK Astronomy Technology Centre and the Institute of Astronomy of Edinburgh University, both highly regarded institutions.

ROYAL OBSERVATORY;

http://www.roe.ac.uk/

2 Keep ahead towards the radio masts. A little way past the second

WHERE TO EAT

🍴 MORNING GLORY,
1 Comiston Road;
Tel: 0131 447 1205.
Located about five minutes from the end of the walk this large bar offers pies and platters, burgers, traditional pub fare and a wide range of sandwiches. ££

one, a short incline brings you to a bench, past which on the right is the viewfinder on the summit of Blackford Hill – prepare for a stunning view.

Blackford Hill, one of the seven hills on which tradition maintains that Edinburgh was built, is formed out of what is reputedly the capital's oldest rock. Although the hill is only 538ft (164m) high, the view that stretches before you in all directions is absolutely stunning. To your right are the Salisbury Crags, which seem to cower beneath Arthur's Seat. Before you the Edinburgh skyline is laid out, dominated by the castle. It is a view to savour, and with the help of the viewfinder, you should be able identify all the landmarks that surround you.

3 Having feasted your eyes on the glorious vista, descend the hill a little way past the viewfinder and head towards the gorse bushes, but turn left just before them and stroll to the steps to the right of the radio mast. Descend them, and at the bottom, go past the bench and left along the path in front of

DISTANCE **3 miles (5km)**

ALLOW **1 hour 45 minutes**

START **Reid Church at West Savile Terrace and Blackford Avenue (bus 41)**

FINISH **Bus stop on Comiston Road**

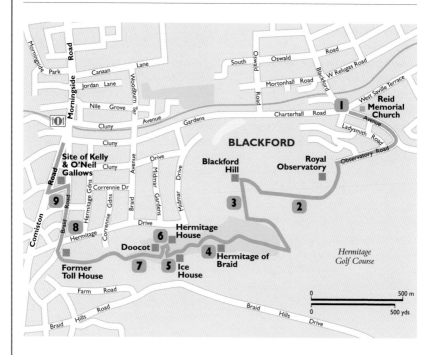

the wall. Follow the path as it bears right and begins a steep descent into a wooded glen, where you head towards the sparkling burn. On reaching the foot of the path, go down the steps turn right and walk under the bridge. Keeping the babbling waters of the burn to your left, enjoy a peaceful stroll through the charming woodland.

You are wandering through the Hermitage of Braid, a designated nature reserve comprising broad-leaved woodland that provides a haven and habitats for an abundance of wildlife. The name is reputedly derived from a hermit's cell that was once situated hereabouts and from the name of Henri de Brad, who owned the area in the 12th century.

HERMITAGE OF BRAID;

www.fohb.org

4 Having crossed several footbridges, the burn should be to your right. Once you've passed a wooden fence (Hermitage House will be on the

opposite side of the burn), go left up the steep steps and pause by the rusting iron gates of the ice house.

In the days before refrigeration the great houses collected ice in winter months from frozen lakes and streams and stored them in these specially constructed chambers. Straw and sawdust would be added between the layers of tightly packed ice to provide insulation and vegetation would be allowed to grow over and around them as a further means of keeping them cold. The ice would be used throughout the summer months to keep food cool, chill drinks, and make ice cream and sorbets.

5 Go back down the steps and cross over to the entrance of Hermitage House, like something out of a fairy tale.

The mock battlements and round corner turrets of this remarkable house resemble a miniature castle. The estate was owned by the De Brad family from 1165 to 1305, after which it passed to the Fairleys, who held it until the 17th century. Wealthy Edinburgh merchant William Dick (1588–1655) owned the estate in the mid-17th century. A staunch royalist and dedicated Covenanter, he provided large amounts of money to King Charles I, for which support he received a knighthood. It then passed through several owners

ABOVE: CLOSE UP OF THE ROYAL OBSERVATORY

and was plundered by Bonnie Prince Charlie's Highland troops in 1745. The estate was purchased by Charles Gordon of Cluny in 1772 and he employed architect Robert Burn to design the present house, which was completed in 1785. In 1938 owner John McDougal gifted the house for use by the citizens of Edinburgh in a public ceremony in front of the house, commemorated by the sundial on the grass in front. Now a visitor centre, it houses an intriguing exhibition on the history and wildlife of the surrounding area.

6 Exit the house and keep ahead past the sundial, crossing the grass and walking past the toilets. Go through the stone gateposts and turn right up the steps to reach the doocot, the Scottish term for dovecote.

This 17th-century sturdy, stone structure is not a particularly attractive building, but it is one of the largest doocots in the Edinburgh area and once contained over 2,000 sandstone nesting boxes. Pigeons were a valuable source of year-round food and this building would have kept

the local laird in fresh meat and eggs. The droppings that inevitably built up inside not only made a good fertilizer, but could also be used in the production of gunpowder and in the leather-tanning and cloth-dyeing processes. With the dawn of the 19th century and the introduction of farming methods that enabled cattle to be fed throughout the winter, the need for doocots began to diminish. Interestingly, doocots are often the only buildings from several great estates to have survived into modern times. Quite why there was an apparent

reluctance on the part of landowners to demolish them is unknown, although it may be connected to the old superstition that the individual responsible for demolishing a doocot would certainly die within the year.

7 Go back down the steps, turn right and follow the path over several flights of steps to turn right on arrival at the asphalt path. Keep ahead through the gate and turn right onto Braid Road, passing the former toll house located on the right.

A memory of the days when those travelling by road into Edinburgh had to pay a toll, this one once stood on the site of Braid Church in Morningside, but was rebuilt here when tolls were finally abolished in 1888.

8 Keep ahead over Hermitage Drive and walk along the left side of the continuation of Braid Road and, having crossed Comiston Terrace, pause on its corner and note the two large stone squares in the road to your right by 66 Braid Road.

These mark the site of the gallows on which, Thomas Kelly and Henry O'Neil were hanged in 1815. The two men's deaths saw Scotland's last execution for highway robbery.

9 Walk along Comiston Terrace at the end of which go right along Comiston Road, cross to its left side and walk to the bus stop where this walk ends.

ABOVE: VIEW OVER WESTERN EDINBURGH FROM BLACKFORD HILL

ARTHUR'S SEAT SEEN FROM BLACKFORD HILL

Literary Legends and the Real Long John Silver

An intriguing and inspiring journey that provides the chance to explore secret Edinburgh at its most exquisite.

This is a lovely and varied walk that brings together magnificent architecture, delightful streets as well as famous, and not so famous, figures from Edinburgh's past. You begin in the district of Stockbridge, a truly beguiling neighbourhood, parts of which were developed by the artist Sir Henry Raeburn (1756–1823). The mid section of the walk takes you past some enchanting houses, where a discreet glance through the windows gives the distinct impression of looking back into a bygone age. By way of one of the most august educational establishments in the city, Edinburgh Academy, you arrive at the birthplace of Robert Louis Stevenson, and a little farther along the former home of the man who inspired the character Long John Silver. The walk ends with the opportunity to take the air and absorb the beauty of the spectacular and admired Royal Botanic Garden, justifiably acclaimed as a jewel in Edinburgh's crown.

The bridge built in 1902 to replace a previous stone bridge over the Water of Leith was constructed in 1786, which helped turn an agricultural backwater into a popular, affluent and sought-after neighbourhood. Cross over to the west side and turn left along Dean Terrace. Stop by the first building immediately on the right.

This is in fact 2 Deanhaugh Street, where Sir James Young Simpson, the discoverer of the anaesthetic qualities of chloroform (see Walk 5), first began practising medicine in a modest first-floor flat.

2 Continue along Dean Terrace past the junction with Carlton Street till you come to St Bernard's Bridge, which dates from 1824. Beyond it is the dome of St Bernard's Well, featured on Walk 9. Keep ahead past Danube Street and ascend Upper Dean Terrace to swing right into Ann Street.

Built between 1816 and 1823, and acclaimed by Sir John Betjeman as 'the most attractive street in Britain', this bucolic thoroughfare is named after Ann Raeburn, wife of the portrait painter Sir Henry Raeburn, the man responsible for developing much of this district. The street comprises some of the most sought-after and expensive residential properties in Edinburgh, most of which, uniquely for the New Town, are set back behind pretty front gardens. On the left, No. 29 was once the home of the poet John Wilson (1785–1854), better known under his pseudonym, Christopher

WHERE TO EAT

⟨1⟩ THE GLOBE DELI,
Corner of Henderson Row and Henderson Place;
Tel: 0131 556 5835.
A selection of sandwiches and wraps, and warming bowls of soup. £

⟨2⟩ DIONIKA,
3–6 Canonmills Bridge;
Tel: 0131 652 3993.
Proud of their reputation for fuss-free cooking, this Spanish restaurant and deli offers a varied menu and also a *tapas* option. £££

⟨3⟩ TERRACE CAFÉ,
Royal Botanic Gardens;
Tel: 0131 552 0606
This café's mission is to source food from local suppliers. Soups, fresh baked breads, quiches and a variety of filling meals. ££

North. Loved and loathed in equal measure by his fellow poets, Wilson was a great friend of Thomas De Quincey, who arrived at this house one night to shelter from the rain and ended up staying for a year. A few doors along, No. 25 was the birthplace of R M Ballantyne (1825–1894), writer of gripping adventure stories. His book *Coral Island* (1858) about three English boys castaway on a South Pacific Island inspired Robert Louis Stevenson's *Treasure Island*, J M Barrie's *Peter Pan* (1904) and William Golding's *Lord of the Flies* (1954).

93

DISTANCE **2.5 miles (4km)**

ALLOW **2 hours**

START **Bridge at junction of Kerr and Saunders streets (buses 24, 29 or 42)**

FINISH **The Royal Botanic Garden**

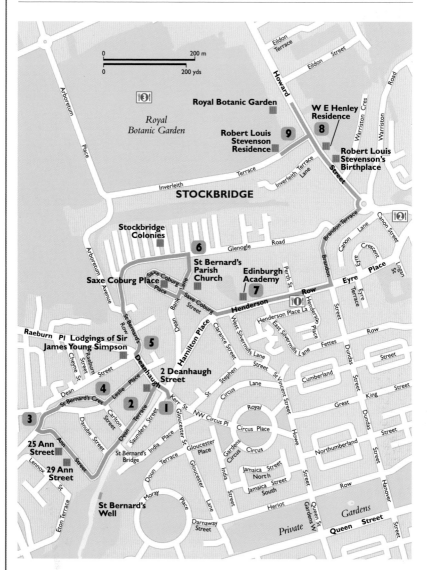

3 At the end of Ann Street, go right along Dean Park Crescent and keep ahead into St Bernard's Crescent, keeping to its left side.

The buildings here contrast sharply with the picturesque, almost understated elegance you have left behind. Its tall houses boast an almost lofty assurance, their bold façades resplendent with soaring Doric columns.

4 Go left into Leslie Place, at the end of which turn left along Deanhaugh Street. Having crossed Dean Street, pause at its junction with Raeburn Place.

It was at a premises at this junction that James Young Simpson lodged with his brother David, who had set up in business here as a baker. At the time he was, according to his own account, 'very, very young and very solitary, very poor and almost friendless'.

5 Cross Raeburn Place via the crossing, then bear right and immediately swing left into St Bernard's Row to follow it as it bears left. Suddenly the urban landscape slips away and the route becomes more rural with each step taken. When the road divides, follow the right fork over the Falshaw Bridge. Walk along Bridge Place and swing right into Glenogle Road.

To your left are 11 parallel terraces known as the Stockbridge Colonies. Laid out between 1861 and 1911 to provide housing for respectable artisans, each of the attractive properties is split into an upper and lower level. The exterior staircases ensured that each tenant could enter their home through their own front door. An intriguing feature is that each row's gable end has a stone carving above the windows depicting the implements and tools of different trades. Today the properties have seen significant gentrification and would be well beyond the means of the average artisan, respectable or otherwise.

6 Having walked a little way along Glenogle Road, go right up the stone stairs opposite Dunrobin Place. Pass between the high walls of Gabriel's Road, bear right into Saxe Coburg Street, go first right and proceed counter-clockwise around Saxe Coburg Place to admire its splendid Georgian properties. Having walked all the way around it, veer diagonally left across Dean Bank Lane, go first right into Saxe Coburg Street, cross to its left side and pause on the left outside St Bernard's Church, dating from 1823. Continue and turn left into Henderson Row, pausing on the left by the gateposts of No. 54.

This was formerly Donaldson's School for the Deaf, but now houses the English and art departments for Edinburgh Academy. It is perhaps best known, however, as the location used as Marcia Blane School for Girls in the film adaptation of Muriel Spark's *The Prime of Miss Jean Brodie*. Next door is The Edinburgh Academy, set up

in 1824 to promote classical learning. The founders, Lord Cockburn and Leonard Horner, were concerned that the standard of Greek taught by the Royal High School was insufficient to compete with the English public schools. The main building, with its Greek Doric frontage, was designed by William Burn (1789–1870). Among the school's early directors was Sir Walter Scott, whilst both R M Ballantyne and Robert Louis Stevenson were pupils here.

EDINBURGH ACADEMY;

www.edinburghacademy.org.uk/

7 Continue along Henderson Row and go left along Brandon Street. Keep ahead into Brandon Terrace, at the end of which go over the crossing and turn left over the bridge into Howard Street. Go over Warriston Crescent and pause on the right outside No. 8 Howard Place, which has the initials RLS emblazoned on its gates.

It was in this house that Robert Louis Stevenson was born on 13 November 1850. The small, cramped two-storey house was plagued by damp, and its proximity to the Water of Leith, into which sewage and the effluent from surrounding mills and tanneries was dumped, created a far from healthy environment. Hence, in 1853, the family moved to the healthier heights of nearby Inverleith Terrace. A few doors along is No. 11, once the home of the poet W E Henley (1849–1903). A friend of and literary collaborator with Stevenson, Henley had had his left leg amputated directly beneath the knee due to tuberculosis of the bone, a fact which influenced Stevenson's creation of Long John Silver in *Treasure Island*. He was also a friend of *Peter Pan* author J M Barrie (1860–1937). Henley's daughter Margaret often referred to Barrie as her 'Fwendy-Wendy', which inspired him to create the character and invent the name Wendy. Sadly, Margaret died in 1894 at the tender age of just four years.

8 Keep ahead, cautiously crossing to the left pavement, and go left into Inverleith Terrace and take a break to look at the outside of No. 9.

It was to this house, overlooking the Botanic Garden, then No. 1, that the Stevenson family moved on 27 June 1853 when Robert was two and a half years old; they remained here until he was seven.

9 Backtrack and go left onto Howard Street. On the left is the East Gate of the Royal Botanic Garden.

Known locally as the 'Botanics', the Royal Botanic Garden is one of the glories of Edinburgh. It contains an extensive and exquisite plant collection and is the second oldest botanic garden in Britain, having originated in 1670 when it was founded as a Physic Garden on a small plot of land near to Holyrood. It moved to its current location in the 1820s and is a place to wander at leisure. On a hill at the centre of the gardens is Inverleith House, a Georgian County home built in 1774 and now used for art exhibitions. Admission to the gardens is free. Having wandered to your heart's content, exit via the East Gate; buses back to the city centre can be taken from the bus stop opposite.

Monarchs, Mariners and Bloodshed

Since 1920 Leith has been part of Edinburgh, but historically the two were separate burghs and Leith still possesses its own distinctive character.

As the major port for access to Edinburgh, Leith has seen many significant events from Scotland's rich and often turbulent past. By 1560, Mary of Guise was ruling Scotland from Leith as regent for her daughter, Mary, Queen of Scots. Her regency ended with French Catholic troops being ousted by Scottish forces aided by English Protestant troops. Her ill-fated daughter would return from France a year later, landing at Leith to begin her six-year reign. Close links with France made Leith Scotland's gateway for the wine trade, and many of the local warehouses were built to hold wine and dry goods, switching in the late 19th century to serve the expanding whisky trade. By the 19th century Leith was a bustling, busy and wealthy port, but the 20th century saw a huge decline in its fortunes and many of its once great buildings fell into disrepair. Today Leith is undergoing a transformation. Although much evidence of its downturn is still visible, old warehouses have been converted into offices and restaurants. The Royal Yacht *Britannia* is berthed here and a major tourist attraction, and it also makes a suitable venue at which to end this fascinating walk.

1 Keep ahead along New Kirkgate and walk through the shopping centre and, having past Farm Foods, pause on the left outside Trinity House.

Although the present building, designed by Thomas Brown, only dates from 1816, Trinity House was founded as a charity on this site in 1555. It was the headquarters of the Incorporation of Masters and Mariners of Leith, which was originally established in 1380 to provide relief for poor, sick and aged mariners. It was funded by a levy on all cargoes passing through the Port of Leith. Now managed by Historic Scotland, it is sometimes open to the public.

2 With your back to Trinity House, go through the gates of South Leith Parish Church.

Built in 1483, the church has had something of a turbulent past. It was looted in 1544 during the 'Rough Wooing'. In 1560, during the siege of Leith, English and Scottish artillery fire destroyed the chancel. The church was extensively remodelled in the 19th century and all that now remains of the 15th-century foundation are the original pillars in the nave.

SOUTH LEITH PARISH CHURCH;

www.slpc.co.uk

3 Leave the church and go left along Constitution Street, passing the Catholic church St Mary's Star of the Sea. Turn left along Queen Charlotte Street and take the second right down

Water Street and, at the junction with Burgess Street you'll see Lamb's House.

Built by merchant Andrew Lamb in the 17th century, Lamb's House stands on the site of a building in which Mary Queen of Scots dined following her arrival in Leith from France in 1561.

4 Go left along Burgess Street. At its end turn left along Shore and keep ahead over Shore Place and Tolbooth Wynd. Having crossed Giles Street, pause by the huge wall on the left. Behind the wall you can see the Vaults, Leith's oldest warehouse, built in 1682, the wine cellars of which date from 16th century.

On the wall a little way along is the Porters Stone, a copy of a 17th-century trade stone that used to be in Tolbooth

DISTANCE **2.75 miles (4.4km)**

ALLOW **2 hours**

START **New Kirkgate at the end of Leith Walk (bus 1, 11, 35 or 22)**

FINISH **Ocean Terminal**

Wynd. There is a representation of a stingman in its top left corner, showing one of the workers whose duties included carrying barrels of wine to taverns and reporting back to the Clerk of Leith how much each one used. The right top corner shows a curious human-powered crane, looking something like a giant

ABOVE: SUNSET VIEW OVER LEITH

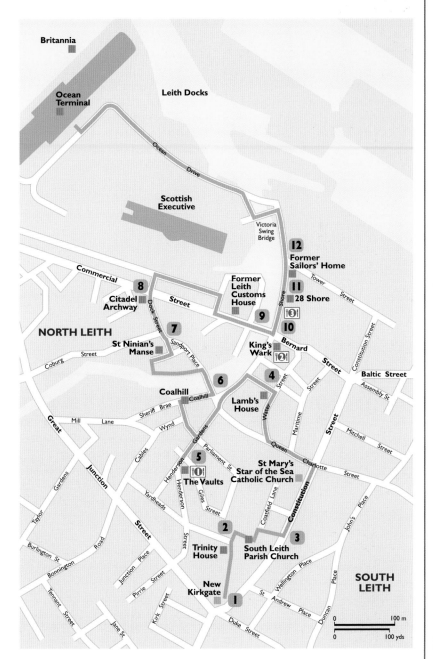

Britannia

Ocean
Terminal

Leith Docks

Ocean Drive

Scottish
Executive

Victoria
Swing
Bridge

12
Former
Sailors' Home

Commercial

8
Citadel
Archway

Street

Former
Leith
Customs
House

Dock Street

11
28 Shore

Tower Street

Shore

9

10

7

NORTH LEITH

St Ninian's
Manse

Sandport Place

Bernard Street

King's
Wark
[2]

Constitution Street

Coburg Street

Mill Lane

6

Coalhill

Coalhill

Sheriff Brae

Wynd

Giles Street

Cables

4

Lamb's
House

Water Street

Maritime Street

Baltic Street

Assembly St.

Street

Mitchell Street

Great

Junction

Parliament St.

5
[o]
The Vaults

Henderson Street

Henderson Street

Queen Street

Charlotte Street

St Mary's
Star of the Sea
Catholic Church

Coatfield Lane

Constitution Street

John's Place

Place

Yardheads

2

Trinity
House

3

South Leith
Parish Church

Wellington Place

St Andrew Place

Duncan Place

**SOUTH
LEITH**

Gardens

Taylor

Burlington St.

Bonnington Road

Junction Place

Pirrie Street

Street

Jane St.

Kirk Street

Tennant Street

1
New
Kirkgate

Duke Street

0   100 m

0   100 yds

WHERE TO EAT

[1] THE VINTNERS ROOMS,
The Vaults, 87 Giles St;
Tel: 0131 554 6767.
Not exactly a walk-in-and-eat place, this elegant dining room is in the old wine merchants' auction room in the historic Vaults warehouse and is a place to splurge at the end of the walk. £££

[2] THE KING'S WARK,
36 The Shore;
Tel: 0131 554 9260.
Candle-lit interior, immensely thick stone walls and a warming fire in winter make this an incredibly atmospheric place. Renowned for its good service and its fantastic food, which ranges from seafood to steaks and vegetarian options. ££

[3] CRUZ,
14 The Shore;
Tel: 0131 553-6600.
Located on a boat moored in Leith port, this sit-down restaurant offers oysters, salads and fresh fish. £££

hamster wheel that was driven by one person, usually a child, walking inside it.

5 Backtrack and go left along Parliament Street, then continue right along Coalhill.

Now lined with modern apartments, this was once one of Leith's most run-down streets and in the 18th century had a reputation for being the haunt of disembodied spirits.

6 Turn left onto Sandport Place, go over the bridge and immediately turn left along the Water of Leith Path. Just after the industrial units, go right through the iron arch and pause on the left outside St Ninian's Manse.

This picturesque building once stood at the head of the first bridge to North Leith, and was first erected by the Abbot of Holyrood in the 15th century, although nothing of that foundation now survives. Rebuilt several times, it was converted for warehouse use in the early 19th century, at which time it was unflatteringly described as 'an unhallowed repository of peas and barley'. Recently converted to offices, its chief glory is the old stair tower, dated 1675, with its eye-catching belfry.

7 Keep straight ahead, veering right to pass between the brown sandstone building and modern grey–white building. Cross over Sandport Place into Dock Street and head towards the church on the left. To its left is the Citadel Archway.

This is part of a huge fortification completed in 1656 by General Monck (1608–1670) as his headquarters after Cromwell placed him in charge of Scotland in the aftermath of the Civil War. However, the restoration of the monarchy under Charles II in 1660

rendered it obsolete and within 10 years it was largely disused and had been partially demolished. It witnessed a brief bout of military service during the 1715 uprising, when it was occupied by the Jacobites. Thereafter the complex was gradually demolished until just this one solitary stone archway remained.

8 Cross over Commercial Street and keep ahead towards the Scottish Government building. Go right along the cobblestone path passing the former warehouse buildings that are now mostly restaurants. Go through the gateposts and walk diagonally right across Dock Place. Go left along Commercial Street and pause on the left outside the former Leith Customs House.

Designed by Robert Reid in 1810, this grand, beautiful building is indicative of how wealthy Leith was in the 19th century. It was here that ship masters would come to declare their cargoes and pay the appropriate duties. Now used as a store by the National Museums of Scotland, there are suggestions at the time of writing that it should become the venue for Leith's museum.

9 Keep ahead over the bridge and pause by the traffic lights to look over at the King's Wark.

First built in 1434 by James I, this was a royal residence, storehouse and armoury. It was destroyed by fire in 1544 when the Earl of Hertford raged through Leith in the course of his 'Rough Wooing' on behalf of Henry VIII. Rebuilt, it became a plague hospital in 1575, and in 1604 James VI gave it to Bernard Lindsay authorizing him to keep four taverns on the site. The present building dates in part from 1702, although it was restored in the 1970s.

10 Go left along Shore, pausing on the right by No. 28, where a fine model ship is seen and where a plaque commemorates the visit of King George IV, who landed at the quayside opposite on 15 August 1822.

Three centuries earlier, on 19 August 1561, Mary, Queen of Scots had also landed at Leith, returning after her childhood years in France. Next door is the Ship Inn, which dates from the 19th century, although it contains the foundation stone from the Old Ship Inn of 1676. In April 1779 a tragic misunderstanding took place at the Ship Inn when 50 Highlanders, who had recently been recruited to the Highland regiments, were sent to embark on a ship in Leith. They mistakenly believed that they had been tricked into joining a Lowland regiment and refused to board the vessel. This effectively made them

mutineers and 200 troops were sent from Edinburgh Castle to take them prisoner. On arrival the major in charge shouted at them in English, which the Highlanders couldn't understand. Panicking, one of the Highlanders fired his weapon and fatally wounded one of the arresting officers. The English troops opened fire and 12 Highlanders were killed.

11 Continue past the Ship, cross over Tower Street and look back at the signal tower, which dates from 1686. Continue and pause a little farther along to look above the door of the large building on the right.

Now a hotel and restaurant, a faded inscription above the door recalls its original use as a sailors' home.

12 With your back to the seamen's home, walk past the sculpture at the centre of the circle of cobbles and go right after the seated statue of Sandy Irvine Robertson, a celebrated 20th-century Edinburgh wine merchant. Keep on past the whale harpoon and follow the walkway, then bear left over the blue Victoria Swing Bridge, completed in 1874. Turn right off the bridge and go left along Ocean Drive. At the end of this road go left at the roundabout and cross over to Ocean Terminal.

Round off your walk here with a visit to the Royal Yacht *Britannia* or enjoy the shops and restaurants in the shopping mall. Buses depart for central Edinburgh from outside the main entrance.

OPPOSITE: THE ROYAL YACHT *BRITANNIA* BERTHED AT OCEAN TERMINAL

Saints, Witches and Evil Omens

A short bus ride from central Edinburgh brings you to some lovely countryside that is steeped in history and mystery.

This is a stirring walk that encompasses gorgeous countryside, historic buildings, a lovely old church, a marvel of Victorian engineering and an intriguing mix of buildings that huddle around a delightful harbour. Early on in the walk you have the opportunity to visit the fascinating and delightful St Cuthbert's Church. Sadly, as with so many historic churches now, St Cuthbert's is obliged to lock its doors as protection from the unwanted attentions of thieves and vandals. Still, if you time your walk to arrive on a weekday mid-morning, you can obtain the key from Dalmeny Post Office at 5 Main Road, on the opposite side of the street, which opens weekdays from 9am to 1pm. From here move on to Dalmeny House, which opens to visitors at certain times of the year, but which can be admired from the outside if closed. Passing a sinister spot that is haunted by a legendary baying hound, look up to see the mighty span of the Forth Railway Bridge, a magnificent feat of Victorian engineering. Finally, by way of a hostelry immortalized by Robert Louis Stevenson, you end your stroll with a wander along South Queensferry's historic High Street.

Turn right along Station Road, pass under the bridge and, having gone over the short road bridge, turn right to descend the steps and turn left. Continue via a pleasant woodland walk and, once under the next bridge, bear left and left again to ascend the grey-railed ramp; at the top turn right along The Glebe. Keep ahead along Dalmeny's Main Street to walk past attractive one-storey cottages. As you pass the village green, cross over to the post office, where you can borrow the key for the church. Cross Bankhead Road and go left through the gates into St Cuthbert's churchyard.

Dating from the 12th century, St Cuthbert's boasts the most complete example of Romanesque architecture in Scotland. The doorway through which you enter is exquisite, its two arches bearing elaborate, though weathered, carvings of fabulous animals, beasts and grotesque heads. A descriptive board inside the church lists what each sculpture is meant to be, and another board guides you around the church's interior. Once inside look up at the rib-vaulted roof and marvel at the solid 12th-century walls, pierced by round Norman windows. Approaching the altar, note the medieval tombs on the floor and the stained-glass window, which was a gift from a Polish airman who was stationed in Scotland during World War II and who fell in love with this pretty little church.

2 Leave the church (remembering to lock up and return the key to the

WHERE TO EAT

[O] THE HAWES INN,
Newhalls Road, South Queensferry;
Tel: 0131 331 1990.
Despite modernization this pub retains some of its old character. The staff are exceptionally friendly, and the food is both good and reasonably priced. The Hawes is a must for all fans of Robert Louis Stevenson, who was a frequent visitor and who immortalized it in *Kidnapped*. £

[O] THE CAFÉ AT DALMENY HOUSE
Tel: 0131 331 1888.
Having trudged up the long drive to Dalmeny House you might be in need of a little refreshment. Thankfully there's a café that does the usual teas and coffes, as well as light snacks and meals. £

[O] PICNIC.
High Street, South Queensferry;
Tel: 0131 331 1346.
Stop off for the teas, coffees, snacks and pastries on offer in this pleasant little local eatery. £

post office) and go left (eastwards) along Main Street out of the village, enjoying the views of the Forth Railway and Road Bridges to your left. Note the old water tower on the right, now converted into a house. At the end of the road keep ahead over the intersecting road and enter the grounds of Dalmeny House. There follows a long stroll along the

DISTANCE 5 miles (8km)

ALLOW 3 hours

START Dalmeny station (train or buses 43, X43 from St Andrews Square)

FINISH Bus stop just past St Mary's Church, South Queensferry

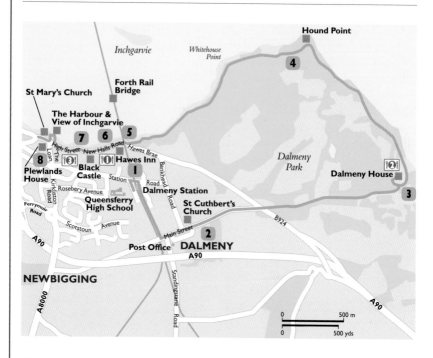

drive, where the vista becomes more rural and secluded with each step.

Eventually you arrive at Dalmeny House itself, a lofty statement in Gothic Tudor architecture completed in 1817 and designed by William Wilkins, who went on to design the National Gallery in London. The house was commissioned by the 4th Earl of Rosebery whose family have owned the Dalmeny estate for over 300 years. Archibald Philip, 5th Earl of Rosebery (1847–1929), was reputed to have had three stated aims in life: to win the Derby; to marry an heiress and to become prime minister. He achieved all three, although his period as prime minister (1894–1895), wasn't particularly happy, and Winston Churchill summed him up as 'the natural leader who never completely accepted the invitation to lead'. The house contains superb collections of furniture, portraits, tapestries and porcelain.

DALMENY HOUSE;

www.dalmeny.co.uk

OPPOSITE: JUBILEE CLOCK IN SOUTH QUEENSFERRY

3 Exit Dalmeny House and turn left after the bronze life-size statue of racehorse, King Tom, who died aged 27 in January 1878. Head down the gentle slope that swings left and go past the woods to keep straight ahead and when you reach a convergence of four keep ahead, following the knee-high Shore Walk sign on the right, marked Queensferry. Go through the white gate and keep ahead until, having passed a single storey cottage on your right, the path ascends and bears left.

Away to your right is Hound Point, which takes its name from the legend of Sir Roger de Mowbray, who headed off to fight in the Crusades. As he was leaving, his faithful hound began to wail so mournfully that Sir Roger was moved

to take it with him. Both of them were killed in battle and on the night they died the baleful howling of a hound was heard echoing around the nearby shore. The hound is meant to be an ill omen for the estate's owners (first the Mowbrays and then the Roseberys), its ghostly baying preceding a death in the family.

4 Casting nervous glances around you, keep ahead on the straight path. The views of the Forth Railway Bridge through the trees to your right are breathtaking and you really get the measure of what a truly massive structure it is, the trains passing over it looking more like models. As the pathway opens out there is another superb view of the two bridges and out across the Firth of Forth.

Work on the Forth Railway Bridge was begun in 1883 and continued over the next seven years. It was the first cantilever bridge in Britain, and the first in Europe to be built of steel. The bridge cost £2.5 million, and 56 of its 5,000-strong workforce died during its construction. It was opened on 4 March 1890 by the Prince of Wales. A strong gale on the day of opening caused consternation but the bridge's engineers dismissed any worries with the words 'a tornado that would uproot trees and devastate a whole countryside would leave the Forth Bridge harmless'. The prince duly travelled out to the bridge's centre on the royal train, climbed down onto the track and hammered in the last of the 6.5 million rivets used in its construction. His rivet was meant to be a gold one, but lack of money meant that a brass one was used instead, although no one confessed this to the prince. Beyond it is the Forth Road Bridge, opened in 1964, at the time the longest suspension bridge in Europe.

FORTH BRIDGES;

www.forthbridge.org.uk

5 Exit the Dalmeny estate via the gate and pass under the Forth Railway Bridge to the Hawes Inn, a 16th-century tavern that retains some of its antiquated character.

The pub was a favourite watering hole of Robert Louis Stevenson, who immortalized it in *Kidnapped* (1886), as the place where David Balfour's wicked and miserly uncle, Ebenezer, arranged the kidnap of his nephew.

6 Leave the inn and go left along New Halls Road. Cross to its right side and keep ahead onto the High Street of the delightful harbour town of South Queensferry. The houses you pass on the left were built for sea captains and traders and date mostly from the 18th century. Pass the interesting Queensferry Museum, and a little farther along on the left is Black Castle.

This is Queensferry's oldest building, dating from 1626. Although it is not a castle, it is most certainly black and its early history is marred by sinister doings. The original owner, a ship's captain, was lost at sea, and his maid found herself accused of paying a beggar-woman to cast a spell against him. Both women were burned for witchcraft.

7 Keep ahead to pass Rosebery Hall and Tolbooth Tower, which has a jubilee clock dating from Queen Victoria's Golden Jubilee of 1887. Go next right along Gote Lane, which brings you to the picturesque little harbour.

In the 17th century, Covenanters hid from the king's troops in the attics of the houses around the harbour. At high tide they embarked on one of the town's fleet of sailing ships and set sail for the more tolerant Low Countries, where they could practise their faith freely. Looking across at the Forth Railway Bridge you can see Inchgarvie, the tiny Island that now acts as a support for the Forth Railway Bridge. Over the centuries the island has been a state prison and a lookout point for pirates. In the 19th century Queensferry was known for its young herring, known locally as garvies, which were salted and exported to Scandinavia and the Netherlands. The island is reputedly named for these fish.

8 Turn left in front of the harbour and go left up Harbour Lane by harbour house. Keep ahead through Bell Stane, then go right onto Hopetoun Road. The large building on the corner to your left is Plewlands House.

This mansion was built in 1641 for Samuel Wilson and his wife, Anna Ponton, and is now owned by the National Trust for Scotland, although it is not open to the public. A little farther along on the right is the lovely church of St Mary's, once part of a medieval Carmelite Friary begun in 1440. The town of Queensferry grew up around it and is named for a ferry established in the 11th century by the saintly Queen Margaret (1046–1093) to transport pilgrims across the Forth to various holy shrines. The church's car park is thought to stand on the site of the original ferry port. A little way past the church is the bus stop from which you can take buses either back to central Edinburgh or to Dalmeny Station.

FORTH RAIL BRIDGE

A Swanston Ramble

Enjoy the lovely landscape as you stroll through the countryside at the foot of Caerketton Hill and explore the picturesque village of Swanston.

Just 5 miles (8km) from Edinburgh's busy city centre lies a pretty little village that the modern age has yet to reach. It offers breathtaking views, fresh country air, plenty of history and connections with Robert Louis Stevenson, who both holidayed here and wrote about it. Indeed the house to which the Stevenson family came to escape from the centre of Edinburgh still exists and forms a highlight of the early section of this walk. But it is by no means the only highlight, for this attractive landscape is littered with them. There is, for example, a wander across the slopes of one of Swanston's two golf courses with enviable views of Edinburgh city centre. But nothing can equal the beauty of the old village itself, where you find yourself surrounded by delightful white, thatched cottages giving the impression that Swanston really is a village that time forgot. Parts of the route can be muddy, so stout footwear is recommended.

Begin at The Hunters Tryst Inn, once a remote roadside inn located far outside Edinburgh.

It is reputedly named for the fact that it was once was a rendezvous, or tryst, for early Scottish kings after hunting on the lower slopes of the Pentland Hills. Today it is a long, low building, surrounded by housing, but still retaining a certain amount of character. According to Robert Louis Stevenson in *Edinburgh Picturesque Notes*, the Hunters Tryst Inn was 'not so long ago haunted by the devil in person. Satan led the inhabitants a pitiful existence. He shook the four corners of the building with lamentable outcries, beat at the doors and windows, overthrew crockery in the dead hours of the morning, and danced unholy dances on the roof. Every kind of spiritual disinfectant was put in requisition; chosen ministers were summoned out of Edinburgh and prayed by the hour; pious neighbours sat up all night making a noise of psalmody; but Satan minded them no more than the wind about the hill-tops; and it was only after years of persecution, that he left the Hunters' Tryst in peace to occupy himself with the remainder of mankind'. The inn was also the meeting point for an athletics group known as the Six Foot Club, whose members used to hold their events in the surrounding fields. Sir Walter Scott and Robert Louis Stevenson were both honorary members.

2 From the inn walk up to the mini roundabout and go left along

WHERE TO EAT

🍴 THE HUNTERS TRYST INN,
97 Oxgangs Road;
Tel: 0131 445 1797.
A pleasant roadside hostelry that, although not ancient in appearance, nonetheless possesses a certain old-fashioned ambience. It offers a varied menu of typical pub food and makes for an ideal venue at which to both start and end your walk. ££

Oxgangs Road, crossing to its right side. Turn first right along Swanston Road, and walk along its left side to cross the bridge over the Edinburgh bypass and keep ahead, passing Swanston Golf Course on the left. When you arrive at a sign for Swanston Farm, go right along that road and keep ahead to pause at the gates of Swanston Cottage, the large white house that you can see ahead.

Note the initials 1880 AC 1893 inscribed above the door of the little cottage by the gates. This was the residence of Alison Cunningham, childhood nurse to the sickly Robert Louis Stevenson, who she would entertain with exciting tales from Scottish history that left him with a lifelong love of storytelling and reading. In 1885 he dedicated *A Child's Garden of Verses* to his beloved 'Cummy'. Built in 1761 as a single-storey building, the upper floor was added about 1835. Between 1867 and 1880 it was leased by Robert Louis Stevenson's parents, Thomas and Margaret, as a summer

DISTANCE **2.5 miles (4km)**

ALLOW **1 hour 30 minutes**

START **Hunters Tryst Inn, Oxgangs Road (buses 4, 16, 18 or 27)**

FINISH **Hunters Tryst Inn, Oxgangs Road**

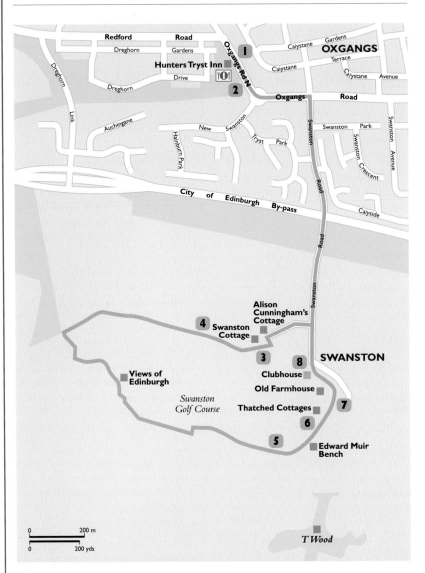

OPPOSITE: THATCHED COTTAGE, SWANSTON

retreat. Stevenson enjoyed long walks in the surrounding hills and his first serious work as a writer was done here. Later in life, he would fondly recall his times at Swanston, and remembering it in his unfinished novel *St Ives*, written in Samoa, where he described it as seeming '…hidden away, being not only concealed in the trees of the garden, but, on the side on which I approached it, buried as high as the eaves by the rising of the ground'.

3 Walk across the stableyard to the left and, just before the stables, go right through the gate to follow the path which goes past Swanston Cottage to the right, which is more visible from here than it was from the gates. A little way after the house's boundary wall ends, go through the next gate onto the golf course and follow the gravel path as it bends right and ascends. Keep ahead when it becomes a grass path and follow it as it swerves left to join another gravel path over a little footbridge and take the right uphill fork.

There might not be a great deal of history on this section, but the views of Edinburgh to your left become more stunning with each step taken, making this section of the walk to truly linger over and an excellent way to keep fit.

4 On arrival at the top of the path bear right and, having passed tee 8, go left up the ascending grass path. Keep ahead over the next green and veer left in front of the unkempt grass bank that goes up to a fence. Follow the path as it swings right and just after the fence ends, go left along the grass and gravel path that passes by trees on the left and gorse bushes on the right. When the path divides keep straight ahead over tee 16, then go down the wooden steps on the left, bear right and keep ahead towards the wooded hill in the distance. The views of Edinburgh are breathtaking, so take the time to absorb this magical vista. At the end of that path tee 12 will be to your right.

On the hillside above is a T-shaped wood planted in 1766 by Henry Trotter of Mortonhall as a memorial to a descendent who fell in battle. It is actually in the shape of a Maltese cross, but when viewed from the hills it looks like a letter T and so is commonly known as T Wood.

5 Keep ahead and, just before tee 12, go left to walk across the green towards the white cottage, just before which go down a dip, and then take the very rough path which begins between two leaning trees and descends a steep grass bank to pick up a narrow grass path that squeezes between the gorse bushes and passes in front of the lovely thatched cottage. Follow the driveway as it twists round the burn and descends to go through the gate.

The bench to the right commemorates the poet Edwin Muir (1887–1959), originally from Orkney, but who loved Swanston and, as the inscription states, would often come to 'linger and meditate' at this peaceful spot.

6 Carry on walking, pausing to admire the lovely thatched, white-washed 18th-century cottages.

Picturesque as they look, these were not particularly desirable residences in the mid-20th century. They had earth floors, no running water and no electricity. A particularly harsh winter in 1947 left the village cut off by huge snow drifts and supplies could only be brought in by horse-drawn plough. But in the 1960s Edinburgh Corporation restored and modernized the cottages and the result is both aesthetically pleasing and seemingly idyllic. They are private homes, so please respect the privacy of the residents.

7 Follow the road as it descends and passes on the left the old school house, which is of uncertain age, and to which children would once travel great distances to receive an education. The school closed in 1931 and the house is now a private residence. Turn right to pass the cluster of small cottages on the

right, built in 1900 to house local farm workers. Go left and follow the road as it descends and swings left, passing the old farmhouse up the hill to your left.

Dating from the 18th century and once the hub of village life, this is still a striking building, and despite being restored following a devastating fire in 1984, an old description of it as being 'old and crow-stepped' still holds true.

8 Go right at the golf club house and keep ahead past the Steadings, a group of mid-18th-century buildings which have now been converted into attractive offices and cottages around a central courtyard. Keep ahead over the Edinburgh bypass, walk along Swanston Road, then go left onto Oxgangs Road. There is a bus stop here but services are limited, so it's best to walk to the mini roundabout and turn right to the Hunters Tryst Inn. There are more regular services back to the centre of Edinburgh from the bus stop here.

Battles, Bloodshed and a Mystical Chapel

This is a lovely walk that encompasses turbulent history and glorious countryside, tinged with just a little mysticism.

The village of Roslin has acquired international fame in recent years thanks to the inclusion of Rosslyn Chapel in the book and subsequent film of Dan Brown's 2003 bestseller *The Da Vinci Code*. But there are many other reasons to explore this magnificent area. The name Roslin is derived from the Celtic words 'ross', meaning a rocky promontory, and 'lynn', meaning a waterfall, and tradition maintains that there has been a settlement here since AD203. In the Middle Ages Roslin became an important seat of the St Clair family and it was they who built its justifiably famous chapel, and the lesser known, now ruinous, castle. It was in Roslin Glen, through which the beautiful North Esk meanders, that the Scots inflicted a resounding defeat on an English army in 1303, and the site of that battle is visited early on in the walk. Thereafter the walk explores the glen, which can get very muddy, so sensible footwear is essential. Having admired the eerie ruins of Roslin Castle the tour ends with a visit to Rosslyn Chapel, where you can marvel at the stunning interior.

Just after the hotel go left along Manse Road. Before you do so you might like to cross over to the war memorial, behind which is a board giving a detailed history of the area. Continue along Manse Road, pass through the bollards. The modern building you pass on the left is the Roslin Bio Centre, the place where Dolly, the world's first mammal to be cloned from an adult cell was born on 5th July 1996. Keep ahead. In the distance to the left you can see the Dryden Tower, a 19th century Gothic folly. Opposite the sign that warns 'Dead slow children and animals', go left passing on the right the cairn that commemorates the Battle of Roslin.

This was caused by a love triangle and fought on 24 February 1303. Edward I's appointed governor in Scotland, Sir John Segrave, had become besotted with Lady Margaret Ramsay, who in turn had fallen deeply in love with Sir Henry St Clair of Rosslyn. In 1302 Segrave learnt that Lady Margaret had consented to marry Sir Henry. Enraged, he asked Edward for permission to invade Scotland and, since the King was already planning a Scottish campaign, he consented. With a force some 30,000 strong Segrave snuck over the border in the dead of one night, and arrived at Melrose in mid-February 1303. Here he made what would prove a major tactical error by dividing his force into three. Alerted by local monks, a numerically inferior Scots army, numbering just 8,000 men headed by Sir Symon Fraser and including Sir William Wallace annihilated the three divisions of

WHERE TO EAT

🍴 **ROSSLYN CHAPEL CAFÉ,**
Rosslyn Chapel;
No phone.
Not a vast place but a nice location at which to enjoy a cup of tea and a snack after you have trudged through Roslin Glen and before you begin your exploration of Rosslyn Chapel. £

🍴 **THE ORIGINAL ROSSLYN HOTEL,**
4 Main Street, Roslin;
Tel: 0131 440 2384.
A pleasant hostelry conveniently located at the start and finish of the tour, which offers pub fare and a relaxing atmosphere. £

the English army in three bloody battles fought on a single day. Segrave was taken prisoner and later ransomed, whilst Sir Henry St Clair enjoyed the victory by spending the night after the battle with Lady Margaret Ramsay.

2 Follow the path, signed for Bilston, as it descends through woodlands, keeping ahead through the two iron gates, and having passed the rusting iron fence on the left, keep ahead over the wooden footbridge, where to your left is Killburn, so called because in the aftermath of the battle its waters are said to have run red with blood for days. At the top of that path bear right, following the sign for Loanhead via Bilston Viaduct. Keep to the path,

DISTANCE **5 miles (8km)**

ALLOW **3–3.5 hours**

START **The Original Rosslyn Hotel (bus 15 from Princes Street)**

FINISH **The Original Rosslyn Hotel**

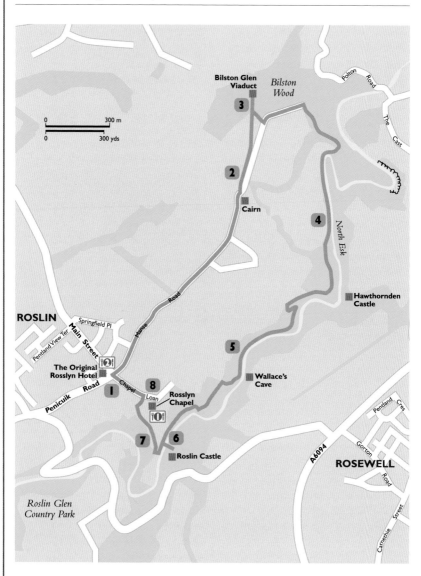

ignoring the uphill path to the left. At the next sign take the track that descends to the right and go left along the intersecting path. Keep going to pass the gap in the wall, passing idyllic woodland. At the next sign go left and walk out onto the spectacular Bilston Glen Viaduct.

Built in 1892 by the North British Railway company, and a true marvel of Victorian engineering with an immense span some 135m (443ft) long, Bilston Glen is the longest lattice-work viaduct in Scotland. The views down into the glen from its midriff are awesome.

3 Backtrack and, just after the sign, go left down the wooden steps on the path between the fences. Go left at the end of that track, wing right, then turn left at the fence and hedge and follow the path until some way along on the right, you arrive at a brown gate signed 'Roslin via riverside path'. Go through that gate and pick up the earth path, following it as it begins a steep descent via a flight of stone steps. When the path divides, go sharp right and on arrival at a drop, go left towards the wooden banister that takes you down a flight of steps. Go left and follow the earth path, passing through two fence posts. From here take the path that swings sharp right through the wooden gate and then twists along the riverside.

Some distance along, having gone over the stepped fence, the path begins a steep ascent and, as it levels off, you can look across at Hawthornden Castle, the earliest parts of which date from the 15th century. In the 16th century it was bought by Sir John Drummond, whose son, the poet William Drummond (1585–1649) was born here. Part of the castle is now used as a writers' retreat.

4 At the junction of two paths, take the right one, which ascends before passing through fence posts, then begins a steep descent down to the river. Keep going, ignoring the first descending left path, but go straight, passing a section of bare rock on the right. Eventually you arrive between two trees, at which point the path divides. Take the left path down towards the river, and edge along the riverside where on the opposite side, you can look up at Wallace's Cave.

The cave resembles a doorway cut out of the rock and is named for William Wallace, although there is no proof that the Scottish patriot ever set foot inside it.

5 Keep ahead along the very narrow, though passable, ledge, which in parts entails cautious scrambling over rocks and boulders. Ascend the rock steps to the right and take the rough earth path that gives lovely views to the river below. When your way is blocked by a large rock, go up the steps to its right. Go right up the next set of steps and follow the path as it climbs and twists through the trees. When it divides, go left fork and keep ahead as it goes uphill and begins a sharp descent towards the river. Follow that path,

down a flight of steps, then keep ahead across an open grass clearing and follow the earth path until the impressive ruins of Roslin Castle loom high over you.

There has been a castle on the rocky promontory since 1304, when the St Clair family sought to strengthen their hold on the surrounding area. Added to over succeeding years, the building was severely damaged by fire in 1447. Rebuilt, it was again burnt down when the Earl of Hertford's forces attacked it during the 'Rough Wooing' of 1544. It

ABOVE: MEDIEVAL DOORWAY, ROSSLYN CHAPEL

was damaged again by General Monck's forces during Cromwell's Scottish campaign of 1650, after which the family built an imposing mansion amidst the ruins. This in turn was sacked by the Edinburgh mob in 1688 owing to the St Clair family's Catholic leanings. Although the house was repaired, it had fallen into ruin by the 18th century, but with parts still habitable. The mansion section was restored in the 1980s and is now available for holiday lets via the Landmark Trust. In addition to a magical, almost fairytale fortress, residents can look forward to making the acquaintance of the White Lady, whose shimmering shade is said to haunt the ruins. They might also hear the baying howls of Roslin's ghostly hound; and if neither of those are sufficient to set the senses tingling, there is always the prospect of the buried treasure reputed to be secreted somewhere amidst the ruins.

6 Step through a gap in the low wall and, just in front of the sandstone arch, go along the path to the left and admire the east façade of the castle, pierced by little slit windows with bars across them. Backtrack, go left under the arch, keep ahead, then go right up the wooden steps as the path ends.

Pause to catch your breath at the top, and look right across the sturdy stone bridge at the castle's courtyard. Go left along the path and follow it as it passes between the cemetery walls. Go right and up the hill, at the top of which turn right. The orangey-brown building on your right is the old inn which has the year 1660

above its door. Dr Johnson stayed here, as did William and Dorothy Wordsworth.

7 Keep ahead, and on the right is the entrance to the Rosslyn Chapel, built by William St Clair, Prince of Orkney, in 1456.

Once inside, prepare to draw breath at an interior that is so rich in ornamental carvings you need time to take in the mystical symbolism that surrounds you. The barrel-vaulted roof is richly adorned with delicate carvings of daisies, lilies, roses and stars. An angelic orchestra is engraved about the walls, but so too are stone demons, saints, martyrs, lions and pagan green men, whilst ferocious dragons coil around intricately carved columns, the most famous of which is known as the Apprentice or Prentice Pillar. This is reputed to have been carved by an apprentice stone mason during his master's absence. When the Master returned he was so envious at the superior skill demonstrated by his pupil that he flew into a rage and struck the unfortunate boy across the head with a mallet, killing him instantly. The chapel features prominently in the final section of *The Da Vinci Code*.

ROSSLYN CHAPEL;

www.rosslynchapel.org.uk

8 Exit left out of the chapel, passing by the old inn. Keep ahead along Chapel Loan to Penicuick Road. Cross over, and on the left, just past the Roslin Glen Hotel, is the bus stop where you can catch a bus back to Edinburgh.

THE MAGNIFICENT INTERIOR OF ROSSLYN CHAPEL

WALK 18

Idylls and Bodysnatchers

A lovely walk along the Water of Leith to the village of Colinton, with its links with Robert Louis Stevenson and associations with bodysnatching.

As you begin this walk you could be forgiven for wondering how it could by any stretch of the imagination be considered lovely. Coming away from the station you find yourself on a noisy, busy and not particularly attractive main road. But persevere, for within minutes you turn onto a woodland track and encounter a delightful section of the Water of Leith Walkway, where the roar of the traffic gives way to the gurgling waters of Edinburgh's river. This section of the walk can be muddy, so stout, sensible shoes are advisable. Having enjoyed the idyllic landscape, the walk takes on an eerie aspect as it passes through the dark Colinton Tunnel, built for the Water of Leith Railway line in the 19th century. However, this spine-tingling section lasts just a few moments before you emerge in a lovely park, through which you make your way to a tranquil churchyard where you encounter chilling tales of bodysnatchers.

1 Leave the station via the exit on platform one. Go down steps and turn right onto Megget Gate, at the end of which turn left along Slateford Road, keeping ahead over Allan Park Road. Pass under the arch of Prince Charlie's Bridge, cross Craiglockhart Avenue and keep ahead along Lanark Road until, just past the bus stop, you go left onto the Water of Leith Walkway.

Before you do, you might like to cross to the opposite side of Lanark Road to the Water of Leith Visitor Centre, located in the 19th-century village school. Here you can see a fascinating exhibition detailing the history and natural resources of the Water of Leith Walkway.

WATER OF LEITH

www.waterofleith.org.uk

2 Keep ahead along the path and as you walk the roar of the traffic is reduced to a distant murmur. Just after a green pipe over the river, the path divides. Take the right fork, passing the delightful, although slightly run down, little grotto on your left.

The grotto dates from around 1750 and is constructed from stones collected from various parts of Scotland. Originally its interior would have been decorated lavishly with shells.

3 Walk over the bridge and follow the path, going up the steps, after which the path descends. As it levels out, turn right over the footbridge. Ahead of you is the Redhall Walled Garden.

Built on the site of the wonderfully named Jinkabout Mill, the garden was constructed in 1758 as the kitchen garden for Redhall House. The name Redhall dates back to the 13th century, and is believed to refer to the original Red Hall Tower, a castle built from local sandstone, which, having been stormed by Cromwell's troops in 1650, was shortly afterwards demolished. Redhall House was built by the Inglis family in the 1750s, and it was they who laid out the riverbanks along which you are walking. There is an information board that gives a brief history of the house and garden.

4 Turn left by the information board and keep ahead through the gate. Take the flight of stone steps and follow the path as it veers left. Just before the division of paths, go left and descend

DISTANCE **4.5 miles (7.25km)**

ALLOW **2 hours**

START **Slateford railway station**

FINISH **Bus stop on Bridge Street, Colinton**

past the bridge to your left. There follows an uphill trudge, after which the path descends and passes through a large grass clearing. Going downhill again, cross another bridge and bear right along the gravel path, passing the white house known as Kate's Mill Cottage – all that survives of a paper mill burnt down in 1890. Veer right, by and on arrival at, the one storey stone cottage bear left, the turn sharp right along the second path and go right to descend a long flight of stairs, at the foot of which bear left along the railed path and go right across the footbridge. Bear right up the long flight of stairs, bear left at the top and keep ahead to enter the eerie and dark Colinton Tunnel.

The tunnel was part of the railway line constructed in the 1870s, which served the mills along the Water of Leith. Easily missed towards the far end of the tunnel on the left is the dark outline of one the Balerno Pug engines specially designed to cope with the particularly steep and twisty route through Colinton Dell.

5 Once through the tunnel keep ahead to pass through the barrier and under the arch of the road bridge. Just before the second barrier, go down the stone stairs to the left of the wall. Keep ahead towards Spylaw House.

Spylaw House was built in 1773 for snuff merchant and tobacconist James Gillespie (1726–1797). Well known for his frugality, Gillespie acquired great wealth. On his death he left his fortune to found a hospital school in Edinburgh, which is still going strong and located in the Marchmont area of the city.

6 Go left over the footbridge then bear left, pass under the road bridge, out of the gates and turn left along Spylaw Street. Keep ahead past the one-storey buildings on the right.

These were originally owned by James Gillespie and may have been built for his own employees. They are now owned by a housing trust and granted free of rent to deserving pensioners.

7 Veer left over the bridge and go right along Dell Road. Pass the modern Church Hall on the left and pause by the gates of Colinton Manse.

Robert Louis Stevenson's maternal grandfather, Lewis Balfour, was the minister at Colinton Parish Church from 1823 to 1860, and the young Stevenson often came to stay. The massive yew tree, in the branches of which the young Stevenson used to play, can still be seen just inside the driveway.

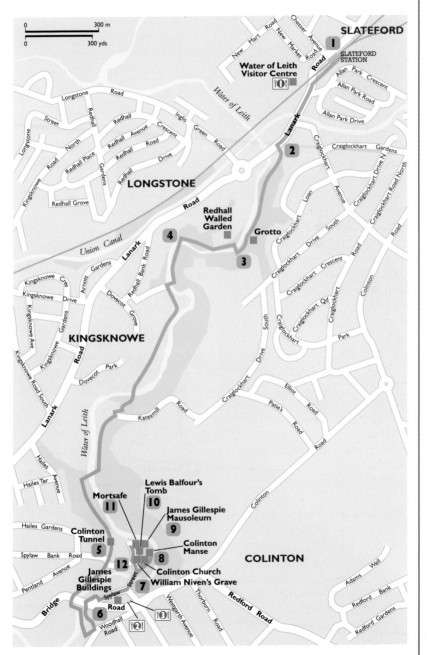

SLATEFORD

1

SLATEFORD STATION

Chesser Avenue
New Hart Road
New Market Road
New Hart Road
Road
Allan Park Crescent
Allan Park Road
Allan Park Drive

Water of Leith

**Water of Leith
Visitor Centre**

Longstone Road

Longstone Street
Longstone Road
North
Redhall
Redhall Place
Redhall Gardens
Redhall Avenue
Redhall Road
Redhall Drive
Redhall
Inglis Green Road
Crescent

Lanark
Road

2

Craiglockhart Loan
Craiglockhart Gardens
Craiglockhart Drive N
Craiglockhart Road North
Craiglockhart Avenue

LONGSTONE

Redhall Grove
Road

**Redhall
Walled
Garden**

Grotto

4

3

Craiglockhart Drive South
Craiglockhart Crescent
Craiglockhart Road
Craiglockhart Qd
Colinton Road

Union Canal

Lanark

Arnott Gardens
Redhall Bank Road

Kingsknowe Cres
Kingsknowe Drive

Dovecot Grove

Craiglockhart Park

KINGSKNOWE

Kingsknowe Gardens
Kingsknowe Ave
Kingsknowe Road
Dovecot Park

Craiglockhart Drive South

Lanark Road

Kingsknowe Road South

Water of Leith

Katesmill Road
Craiglockhart Road

Elliot Road
Patie's Road

Road

Hailes Avenue
Hailes Ter

Colinton Road

**Lewis Balfour's
Tomb**

Mortsafe

11

10

**James Gillespie
Mausoleum**

9

Hailes Gardens

**Colinton
Tunnel**

5

**Colinton
Manse**

Spylaw Bank Road

8

COLINTON

Pentland Avenue

12

**James
Gillespie
Buildings**

Colinton Church

7

William Niven's Grave

Adams Well

Redford Bank

Bridge

6

Spylaw
Road

Woodhall
Road

Westgarth Avenue
Thorburn Road

Redford Road

Redford Gardens

131

WHERE TO EAT

🍴 **WATER OF LEITH VISITOR CENTRE,**
24 Lanark Road;
Tel: 0131 455 7367.
The visitor centre has a pleasant little café, offering teas and coffees and light bites. £

🍴 **COLINTON INN,**
12 Bridge Rd;
Tel: 0131 441 3218.
Having trudged through the decidedly eerie Colinton Tunnel you might feel in need of a wee dram to steady the nerves. The pub also serves traditional pub food. £

🍴 **FANELLI'S DELICATESSEN,**
Bridge Road;
Tel: 0131 441 5844.
Rolls, sandwiches, teas and coffees are on offer at this basic deli located at the end of the walk. £

8 Backtrack a little, turning right up the steps by the church hall and walking into the churchyard.

There has been a church on this site since at least 1248, though the medieval church was razed by the Earl of Hertford's invasion force during the Rough Wooing of 1544. The church was rebuilt, then altered and extended several times before being rebuilt in 1908. Surrounded by a modern function hall and offices that were built in 1998, the church doesn't have an antiquated feel about it, but the churchyard that surrounds it positively brims with tombstones, and holds more than a few surprises for those who care to explore.

Follow the path as it bears left and pause by the iron mortsafe, a grim reminder of a sinister past. This is the only one that remains of six such mortsafes that the church was forced to purchase in the 1820s to keep newly buried parishioners safe from the unwanted attentions of the 'resurrectionists' or bodysnatchers, who, if they could, would dig them up and sell them to Edinburgh's medical fraternity. The ordinary wooden coffin would be placed inside the mortsafe and buried as normal. Once the body had decomposed it would be exhumed, the mortsafe recovered to be used again and what remained of the corpse would be reinterred. This particular mortsafe weighs approximately 1,000kg (2,200lb), and given the frequent use it was put to over the years, is in surprisingly good condition!

9 Go clockwise around the church and, as you arrive at the bench, look left at the leaning tombstone of William Niven, 'weaver in Slatefoord'.

Read the inscription on the reverse side of the tombstone which reminds us that:

*'Death's a Dett
To Nature Deeu
I Have Paid it
So Mon you.'*

OPPOSITE: EARLY MORNING FROST BY THE WATER OF LEITH

10 Continue along the path and go right, passing on the left the large mausoleum of James Gillespie.

The next tomb along is that of the Reverend Lewis Balfour, who his grandson Robert Louis Stevenson described as 'a man of singular simplicity of nature; unemotional, and hating the display of what he felt; a lover of his life and innocent habits to the end'.

11 Backtrack along the path and go right at the mortsafe.

The small box-like building on the left was used to keep a nocturnal watch over the churchyard lest the bodysnatchers should attempt to desecrate a fresh grave. Note the sinisterly leering skull and cross bones on the gravestone against its wall.

12 Go left out of the gates, walk back over the bridge and keep going to the end of Spylaw Street to cautiously cross over Bridge Road.

Pause on the opposite side to admire the iron railings and gates by Phoebe Anna Traquair (1852–1936), a Colinton resident who was a leading figure in the Scottish Arts and Crafts Movement and the first important professional woman artist of modern Scotland. A little further along Bridge Road is a bus stop for the trip back to central Edinburgh.

Writers, Rogues and Sherlock Holmes

This is a walk of real contrasts, from brash, modern Edinburgh to the mellow old city, passing points of interest with literary associations.

You begin amidst the ugly spread of Edinburgh's modern St James's shopping centre. Following a visit to a magnificent cathedral you encounter the ultimate thrill for mystery seekers, the birthplace of Sir Arthur Conan Doyle, creator of the world's most famous detective, Sherlock Holmes. Although the house in which he was born no longer exists, the auspicious event is remembered by a statue of his creation. Your way then lies through a veritable warren of lovely old Edinburgh streets encountering such historical figures as Marie Stopes, J M Barrie and Compton Mackenzie. This section shows off New Town Edinburgh at its finest and most picturesque and should be taken at a slow pace to get the real sense of its beauty. This is Edinburgh's best Georgian architecture. Having encountered a massive church, the proportions of which will really take your breath away, you arrive at the childhood home of Robert Louis Stevenson. Finally, by way of some delightful, old, tucked-away mews you find yourself on Princes Street to be greeted once more by the rush of modern Edinburgh.

With your back to the Wellington Statue go left, then left again down Leith Street, keeping ahead over Little King Street. On the left is St Mary's Metropolitan Cathedral.

The cathedral was originally built in 1801 as a Catholic chapel by Bishop George Hay after a mob had destroyed his former chapel in Edinburgh's Old Town. Hay hoped that the surrounding shops and tenements would keep his new foundation hidden from view and thus spare it a similar fate. It became a cathedral in 1886 and was gradually expanded and remodelled to the extent that only the Gothic façade of the original building survives. An information board to the right of the doors provides a more detailed history. Its interior is very colourful and is worth a visit if open.

ST MARY'S EPISCOPAL CATHEDRAL;

www.stmaryscathedral.co.uk

2 Leave the cathedral, go left off the steps and pass the Conan Doyle pub. Go over the two sets of lights and veer right into Picardy Place. A plaque on the wall of No. 2 commemorates the fact that Arthur Conan Doyle, the creator of Sherlock Holmes, was born at 11 Picardy Place, which stood opposite. Farther on the right is an imposing statue of Sherlock Holmes.

Arthur Ignatius Conan Doyle (1859–1930), the creator of the world's most famous detective, was born into a quite poor Anglo-Irish Catholic family. His father, Charles Altamont Doyle, a

WHERE TO EAT

⊙ THE CONAN DOYLE PUB,
71–73 York Place;
Tel: 0131 524 0031.
Since it stands close to the birthplace of Sir Arthur Conan Doyle, whose name it bears, this comfortable pub contains bits and pieces of memorabilia pertaining to his most famous creation, Sherlock Holmes. A portrait of a genial-looking Conan Doyle welcomes you and stills from various Holmes movies adorn the walls. Usual pub grub and ales. £

⊙ THE STAR BAR,
1 Northumberland Place;
Tel: 0131 539 8070.
The pub has a grisly relic in its cellar in the form of a human skull that no one dares remove, since everyone who has attempted to do so has died soon afterwards. This is great little bar, not plush, but certainly packed with character. The food – available all day – is basic but filling. £

talented artist, was a chronic alcoholic, prone to depression and epilepsy, and he was eventually institutionalized. His mother, Mary, was desperate to keep the young Arthur away from his father's destabilizing influence, and in 1868 the nine-year-old Doyle was sent to a Jesuit boarding school in England. He later returned to study medicine at Edinburgh, where he was tutored by the charismatic and brilliant Dr Joseph Bell, on whom

DISTANCE **2.5 miles (4km)**

ALLOW **2 hours**

START **Wellington Statue on Princes Street, outside West Registry House**

FINISH **Princes Street**

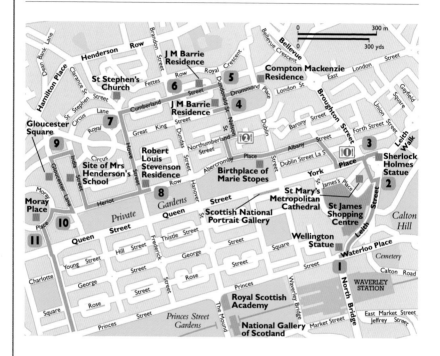

he partly based Sherlock Holmes. In March 1886 Conan Doyle began writing a story entitled *A Tangled Skein*, featuring the characters Sherringford Holmes and Ormond Slacker. Wisely, he later changed the title to *A Study in Scarlet* and the protagonists' names to Sherlock Holmes and Dr Watson. After several rejections, the story appeared in the 1887 *Beeton's Christmas Annual* and was received favourably enough to justify its own separate edition the following year. Interestingly, publication included six pen-

and-ink drawings sketched by Charles Doyle, who at the time was confined in a psychiatric institution in Edinburgh. Evidently the father recognized some of his own character in his son's creation as his sketches depicted Holmes as bearing an uncanny resemblance to himself.

3 Backtrack along Picardy Place and keep ahead over Broughton Street into York Place. Take the first right into York Lane as modern Edinburgh slips farther behind with each step. Go left

IN MEMORY OF
SIR ARTHUR CONAN DOYLE
BORN ON 22 MAY 1859 CLOSE TO THIS SPOT
DONATED TO THE CITY OF EDINBURGH BY
EDINBURGH AND LOTHIANS BRANCH OF THE FEDERATION OF MASTER BUILDERS
ON THE FEDERATIONS 50TH ANNIVERSARY

UNVEILED ON 24 JUNE 1991 BY
PROFESSOR GEOFFREY D. CHISHOLM
CBE, FRCS.Ed, FRCS.Eng, FRCP.Ed, FRACS(Hon), F.CS(SA)(Hon)
President, The Royal College of Surgeons, Edinburgh

into Albany Street, keep ahead over Dublin Street into Abercromby Place, and pause on the left outside No. 3, where a plaque remembers Marie Stopes (1880–1958), birth-control pioneer and prolific author who was born here. Cross to the right side of Abercromby Place, which has the distinction of being the first curved street in Edinburgh. Go first right into Nelson Street and turn right into Northumberland Place. Follow it left into the continuation of Nelson Street to go next left into Great King Street, pausing outside No. 3.

The author J M Barrie (1860–1937), author of the timeless classic *Peter Pan*, lodged here when he was a struggling young journalist. His landlady, Mrs Edwards, was the inspiration for his short story *The Old Lady Shows Her Medals*.

4 Retrace your footsteps, go left and follow Drummond Place as it bears right. Cross over Scotland Street and pause by No. 31.

This was the home of author Sir Compton Mackenzie (1883–1972), best known for his Hebridean comedies *Whisky Galore* and *Monarch of the Glen*.

5 Go back over Scotland Street, right into Dundonald Street and first left into Cumberland Street. Cross to its right side and pause outside No. 14.

J M Barrie lodged in a top-floor flat here with his brother Alec while studying at Edinburgh University.

6 Keep ahead over Dundas Street to follow the continuation of Cumberland Street, at the end of which go left along St Vincent Street. As you do so, look right to take in the vast façade of St Stephen's Church.

Completed in 1828, and designed by William Henry Playfair (1789–1857), the church was once described, rather unjustly, as 'a mouth without cheeks'. The church has a massive square tower of 160ft (48m) high and its cavernous interior was

designed to accommodate a congregation of 1,600 people. The church was divided in two in the 1950s and it now operates as a community centre.

7 Keep ahead over Great King Street and walk along Howe Street to go left along Heriot Row. Three doors along on the left is No. 17, the childhood home of Robert Louis Stevenson from 1857 until 1880.

His room was the one on the far right of the top floor, and here the sickly Stevenson was cared for by his devoted nurse Alison Cunningham, 'Cummy' as she was known to the family. Confined to the house by frequent illness, Robert would read profusely, whilst Cummy would hold him enthralled with tales of ghosts and ghouls, of Scottish history, and the bible. As night fell he would look down from the window and await the arrival of Leerie the lamplighter, whom he later remembered in *A Child's Garden of Verse*, a quote from which is inscribed on the railings beneath the handsome lamp that still adorns the property:

*'For we are very lucky with a lamp
  before the door
And Leerie stops to light it as he lights
  so many more.
And O! before you hurry by with ladder
  and with light.
Oh Leerie see a little child and nod
  to him tonight.'*

It is possible to stay at the property as it offers bed and breakfast and the chance to make the acquaintance of Stevenson, whose ghost is believed to haunt it.
STEVENSON HOUSE;
www.stevenson-house.co.uk

8 Backtrack to cross over Howe Street, keep ahead along Heriot Row and go first right into India Street, crossing to its left side.

No. 36 on the left was Mrs Henderson's School, which Robert Louis Stevenson attended between 1858 and 1861, before moving to Edinburgh Academy.

9 Go next left into Gloucester Place, then left again into Gloucester Lane.

The street is lined with properties that were built to store the carriages and stable the horse of the great houses roundabout. Be sure to take a detour right into Gloucester Square to admire the quaint 19th-century properties that surround it – desirable residences now.

10 Turn right into Darnaway Street and then left into Moray Place, part of the last phase of the New Town.

New Town was begun in 1822 when the Earl of Moray began developing his estate here. With is its original appearance it has become a favoured film location.

11 Go left into Forres Street, cross over Queen Street via the lights, keep ahead into North Charlotte Street and eventually arrive back at Princes Street, where this walk ends.

139

A Treasure Island and a Timeless Village

Despite being under the flight path to Edinburgh Airport, the sleepy village of Cramond has remained relatively untouched by the modern age.

This is a lovely walk that begins in a sleepy churchyard before entering the grounds of an 18th-century house to gaze upon Roman remains. As you go in a peaceful wood, you pass by one of the oldest sites of human habitation in Scotland, before emerging into the harbourside village of Cramond, where you can visit a favoured haunt of Robert Louis Stevenson, the Cramond Inn. Suitably refreshed you can then, if the tide is out, walk across the causeway to explore Cramond Island. With its abandoned World War II fortifications and buildings, this is undoubtedly a highlight of the walk, but be sure you check the times of the tides before making the trek out to it. It is suggested to time your walk to ensure the island is accessible and you can get the times of low tides by phoning (tel: 01333 450666). Once back on the mainland, you explore the harbour and then enjoy a peaceful woodland stroll to the ruins of an old house that feature in one of Edinburgh's famous legends. The going can be very muddy so stout footwear is essential.

1 Walk along Cramond Glebe Road (a sign points towards the village) passing the Manse on the right. On the opposite side of the road is the Old Schoolhouse, built in 1778 and now a private residence.

A little farther along go right through the gates of Cramond Kirk, and enjoy for a few moments the idyllic tranquillity of this lovely spot, though your enjoyment might be curtailed by the frequency of planes heading to land at nearby Edinburgh airport. The first building on the site of Cramond Kirk was a Roman fort built in AD142, and when the Romans left, a Christian community began using the main block as a place of worship. The oldest part of the current building is the tower, which dates from the 15th century, whilst the rest of the kirk was added over subsequent centuries. The bell, which rings out to announce the 11am service on Sundays, dates from the 17th century and was cast in Holland. When Cromwell's forces invaded Scotland in 1650 his soldiers looted and made off with the kirk's bell. However, following a heartfelt plea from the church officers, General Monck agreed to its return.

CRAMOND KIRK;

www.cramondkirk.org.uk

2 Exit right out of the kirkyard and go next right through the gates of Kirk Cramond, where you can see markers for the Roman fort on the right.

The fort was first built in the AD140s and rebuilt in AD208 after the African-born Emperor Septimius Severus launched the last major campaign of Roman conquest in Scotland. Severus not only wished to quash the northern Caledonian tribes that were laying waste the north of Roman Britain, but he also wanted to give his two sons, Geta and Caracalla, a taste of army discipline away from the luxuries of Rome. His campaign, however, was short lived, as he died at York in 211, after which Caracalla murdered his brother, paid off the enemy and headed back to the pampered life in Rome. The fort at Cramond thereafter fell into disuse.

3 Keep ahead along the path. Cramond House is ahead to the right.

The central portion was built in the 1680s, the classical façade was added in 1778 and the rear section was completed in 1820. Queen Victoria's mother, the Duchess of Kent, took over the house in 1860 and was visited here by her daughter en route to Balmoral. The house is now owned by Cramond Kirk and used by the Scottish Wildlife Trust as their headquarters. To the left of Cramond House is Cramond Tower, a fine example of a medieval Scottish defensive tower that was once owned by the Bishops of Dunkeld before being bought by the Ingliss family in 1622. It was they who built Cramond House in 1680 after which the tower was abandoned and over the next 300 years was allowed to fall into ruin. Restored in the 1970s, the tower has been transformed into an imposing private residence.

DISTANCE **3 miles (4.8km)**

ALLOW **2 hours**

START **Junction of Cramond Road North/Cramond Glebe Road (bus 41)**

FINISH **Bus stop outside the Cramond Brig Hotel on the A90**

4 Backtrack and, opposite the third tree on the left, go right along the earth path to descend through the woodland. As the path veers sharp left, pause by the information board, which gives details of Mesolithic Cramond.

In 1995 the remains of what was at the time Scotland's oldest settlement were discovered beneath the overgrown and unkempt ground ahead of you. Finds included numerous burnt hazelnut shells as well as pits and postholes, which suggested this had been a hunter-gatherer encampment dating from between 8630BC and 8250BC. Thus the unsightly tangle of woodland and bracken that lies

before you is probably one of the oldest sites of human occupation in Scotland.

5 Keep ahead past the information board where, again now overgrown, are the best preserved remains of a Roman bathhouse in Scotland, discovered in 1975. Keep ahead and, having passed through a tunnel of trees, go down the steps and through the two posts and proceed ahead and left into Cramond Village.

A little way along on the right is the 17th-century Cramond Inn, a favoured haunt of Robert Louis Stevenson when he was a young man, and today haunted by a spectral woman of unknown identity who has been known to follow staff as they walk through the pub. In parts the inn is extremely atmospheric and makes for a well-earned respite from your ramble with a drink and a bite to eat.

6 Turn right out of the inn, follow the road as it bears left, then go right and keep ahead to pass to the left of the flagpole.

Ahead of you is the causeway, which at low tide leads out to Cramond Island. The island is only accessible at certain times of the day so, before attempting the crossing, it is essential to check the board

ABOVE: ROMAN SOLDIER PORTRAYED ON THE CRAMOND INN SIGN

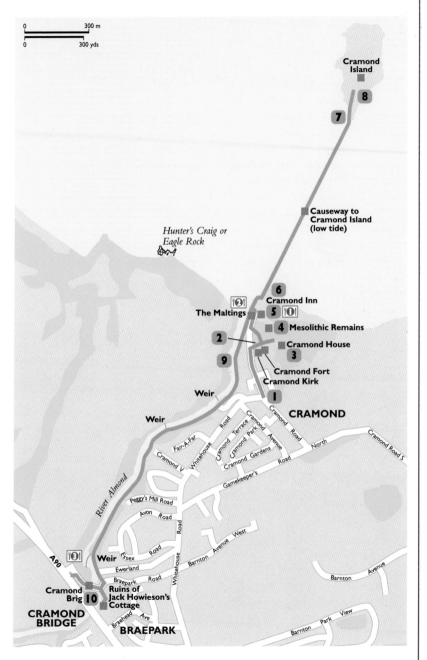

0 300 m
0 300 yds

Cramond
Island

8

7

Causeway to
Cramond Island
(low tide)

*Hunter's Craig or
Eagle Rock*

6

Cramond Inn

The Maltings   **5**

4 Mesolithic Remains

2   **3** Cramond House

9

Cramond Fort
Cramond Kirk

Weir

1

Weir   CRAMOND

Fair-A-Far
Cramond Terrace
Cramond Park
Cramond Gardens
Cramond Avenue
Cramond Road
Whitehouse Road
Cramond V
Cramond Road North
Cramond Road S

Gamekeeper's Road

Peggy's Mill Road

Avon Road

Whitehouse Road

River Almond

Essex Road

Barnton Avenue West

Barnton Avenue

A90

Weir

Ewerland

Braepark Road

Cramond
Brig   **10**

Ruins of
Jack Howieson's
Cottage

Braehead Ave

**CRAMOND
BRIDGE**

BRAEPARK

Barnton Park View

that gives tidal information, and be sure that you have at least an hour to cross, explore the island, and return.

7 Having crossed the mile-long (1.6km) causeway, scramble up the rocks to the right and explore the World War II gun emplacements.

Like many islands in the Firth of Forth, Cramond was fortified during World War II as protection against enemy warships. If you cross to the far side of the island the abandoned store rooms, shelters and further gun emplacements, some with rusting iron doors hanging

off their hinges, can be very eerie indeed. The island was reputedly the inspiration for Robert Louis Stevenson's *Treasure Island* and is imbued with a genuine sense of timeless mystery.

8 Walk back over the causeway, proceed to the right of the flagpole, and keep ahead following the low harbour wall.

The Maltings, the tall white buildings to your left, are surmounted by a large number of chimneys. This is because they once provided housing for local workers and each family had its own room with

their own cooking facilities and fireplace. Pause a little farther along on the right by the steps down to the harbour. This is where the Cramon Lioness, one of Britain's most important Roman sculptures, was discovered in the harbour mud in 1997. In The Maltings to your left is the headquarters of the Cramond Heritage Trust, where an exhibition showing the history of the village can be visited at weekends.

CRAMOND HERITAGE TRUST;

www.cramondheritagetrust.org.uk.

9 Go through the boatyard and into the woodland to join the River

WHERE TO EAT

⊙ CRAMOND INN,
30 Cramond Glebe Road;
Tel: 0131 336 2035.
Situated a stone's throw from the picturesque harbour, this lovely old pub offers filling meals, a pleasant atmosphere and reasonable service. £

⊙ CRAMOND GALLERY BISTRO,
5 Riverside;
Tel: 0131 312 6555.
Situated in the Maltings on Cramond Harbour, this is a lovely little café, the wall of which is adorned by a massive painting of Cramond Fort. The café serves teas, coffees and a selection of hearty home-made dishes. £

⊙ CRAMOND BRIG HOTEL,
Tel: 0131 339 3450.
A roomy place where you can enjoy a restorative pot of tea or coffee at the end of your walk, or tuck into a more substantial meal such as chicken curry, kebabs, and traditional pub fare and drinks. £

Almond Walkway. Follow the path through woodlands and across the car park into the next woodland section. Past the ruins of Fairafar and Niddry Mills, go up the steps and look down to your right at the weir. Continue along the riverside path to ascend the stairs, which you come to on the left. These lead to a delightful cliff-top walk before descending the stairs on the other side.

145

Keep ahead along the path until it divides, then take the left fork and walk along Dowie's Mill Lane. Turn right at the end of the lane and, before the white cottage on the left, go left through the gap in the walls. Keep along, following the path as it swings right and, just after the incline, go right down the flight of steps to the river.

On the left are the ruins of Jock Howieson's Cottage. According to legend, Jock Howieson (or Howison) was a poor tenant farmer who one day went to the rescue of a man who was being assaulted by a gang of ruffians on the nearby brig (bridge). Having fought off the attackers, he brought the man back to his cottage to treat his wounds and give him time to recover from the ordeal. It transpired that the man was in fact King James V (1512–42), and the grateful monarch

rewarded Howieson by granting him possession of the farm he tenanted. The only condition was that Howieson and his descendents must wash the monarch's hands whenever he crossed over the brig, a custom that was later revived by Sir Walter Scott when George IV visited Edinburgh in 1822.

10 Backtrack to the white cottage. Go left past it and onto the brig itself, which has been in use since 1500.

Halfway across on the left you can see carved into the stone the various years in which the brig has been repaired. It was here that Jock Howieson reputedly saved the life of James V. Once over the brig, go up the hill and left across the Cramond Brig Hotel car park and you will find a bus stop from where you can catch a bus back to central Edinburgh.

OPPOSITE: ON THE WATER AT CRAMOND ABOVE: CRAMOND VILLAGE

Fine Architecture and a Famous Detective

In the magnificent streets and lovely crescents of the New Town you will encounter some famous figures from bygone Edinburgh.

The rush of modern Edinburgh is never far away on this walk, yet the streets through which you traipse have succeeded in keeping it well and truly at arm's length. Beginning with the house where Alexander Graham Bell, the inventor of the telephone, was born, you enjoy a circuit of one of the finest Georgian squares in existence. Here you have the opportunity to visit the magnificent Georgian House, restored by the National Trust for Scotland, and inside which you can really get a feel for what it was like to live in the New Town in its early years. The house is only open between April and October and closes at 5pm, so if doing the walk between those months ensure that you allow enough time to comply with its opening hours. But even if you do the walk at other times of the year there is plenty to delight: the house where Dr Joseph Bell was living when his former pupil, Arthur Conan Doyle, based Sherlock Holmes on him and a breathtaking church that really does dominate the Edinburgh skyline.

1 Walk along the left side of South Charlotte Street and pause outside No. 14, just before the traffic lights. This was the birthplace of Alexander Graham Bell (1847–1922).

His mother began going deaf when he was 12 and this had a profound effect on the young Bell, who began developing various systems to help her understand conversations. These included a method of tapping out what was being said with his finger. In 1863 Bell and his brother created a realistic talking skull which delighted the neighbours with its ability to say 'Mama'. Alexander then learnt to manipulate the family's Skye terrier's lips and vocal chords in such away that it appeared to talk. As an adult Bell continued his research into speech and hearing and experimented with several hearing devices, which culminated in his greatest invention – the telephone, although he refused to have one in his study.

2 Go left into Charlotte Square and walk around it clockwise.

Charlotte Square was the last part of the first section of the New Town and was completed in 1820. Much of its design was done by Robert Adam (1728–92), who died just as work commenced. It is a magnificent epitaph to him and its buildings are exquisite. Whigwam's Wine Cellars on the next corner along occupy the house (24 Hope Street) where Earl Haig, Commander of the British forces on the Western Front during World War I, was born in 1861.

WHERE TO EAT

101 NATIONAL TRUST FOR SCOTLAND CAFÉ,
28 Charlotte Square;
Tel: 0844 4932100.
Situated in a magnificent Georgian building, this café offers light lunches, Scottish home-baked cakes and bread, not to mention 'famously good coffee'. ££

102 CORNERSTONE CAFÉ, ST JOHN'S CHURCH,
3 Lothian Road;
Tel: 0131 229 0212.
A range of home-made dishes including pies and pastries, as well as warming soups are offered at this pleasant little eatery beneath the church where your walk ends. £

103 THE OLIVE TREE CAFÉ,
St. George's West Church;
Tel: 0131 225 7001.
A bustling café that offers a range of dishes ranging from tasty vegetarian options as well as soups and sandwiches. £

3 Cautiously cross Hope Street and continue walking clockwise around Charlotte Square.

You pass West Register House on the left, formerly St George's Church and now owned by the National Archives.
NATIONAL ARCHIVES OF SCOTLAND;
www.nas.gov.uk

OPPOSITE: A BEDROOM SCENE IN THE GEORGIAN HOUSE

NCE 2 miles (3.2km)

w 1 hour 45 minutes

START **Junction of South Charlotte Street and Princes Street**

FINISH **St John's Church, Lothian Road**

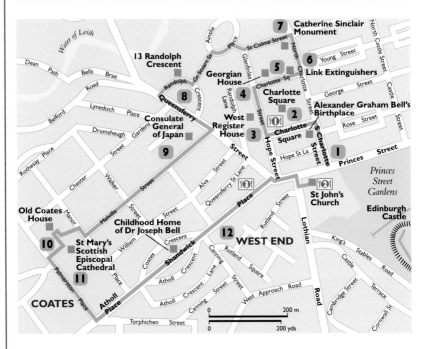

4 **Continue walking round the square until you arrive at No. 7.**

The Georgian House was fully restored by the National Trust for Scotland and part of a row of what are arguably the finest Georgian properties in Edinburgh. The house gives a vivid insight into how the monied classes lived in the New Town in around 1800. For contrast take a look at life below stairs.

GEORGIAN HOUSE;

www.nts.org.uk/Property/56/

5 **After your visit leave the house and turn left, noticing the link extinguishers on the railings at the entrances to the houses.**

These were once used to extinguish the torches, or links, carried by the linkboys who escorted carriages and sedan chairs through the streets of Edinburgh by night. Since 1999, Bute House, at No. 6, is the official residence of the first minister, the head of the devolved Scottish government.

150

OPPOSITE: GEORGIAN ELEGANCE ON GLENFINLAS STREET

6 Go left down North Charlotte Street and pause just before the next traffic lights, where on the left is the Catherine Sinclair monument.

Catherine Sinclair (1800–64) was a prolific writer whose output included children's books, light romances and travel guides. She was also a great philanthropist, establishing workers' canteens, setting up the first fountain in Edinburgh and funding street benches. When she died hundreds of people lined the streets to pay their last tributes as the funeral cortege headed for St John's church, where she is buried.

7 Turn left onto St Colme Street, keep ahead over Glenfinlas Street, veer right on the opposite side and turn left into Ainslie Place. Follow it left into Great Stuart Street and turn right into Randolph Crescent.

No. 13 on the right has a plaque on its wall to the Stevenson sisters Louisa (1835–1908) and Flora (1829–1904), campaigners for women's suffrage, university education for women, and effective, well-organized nursing.

8 Go left along Queensferry Street keep ahead past the bus stop, cross over Randolph Crescent and then turn right into Melville Street, keeping ahead along its right side, go over Melville Crescent and pause outside No. 2.

Now the Consulate General of Japan, from 1884 to 1911 it was the home of

Dr Joseph Bell. It was while Bell was living here that, in 1887, his former pupil and out-patient clerk, Arthur Conan Doyle, penned the first of his Sherlock Holmes adventures, *A Study in Scarlet*, basing his soon-to-be-immortal sleuth on his old tutor. In 1892 Conan Doyle dedicated *The Adventures of Sherlock Holmes* to Bell and wrote to him, 'It is most certainly to you that I owe Sherlock Holmes'.

9 Turn left in front of No. 2 and bear right to walk along the continuation of Melville Street. Keep ahead over Manor Place and gaze up at the magnificent St Mary's Scottish Episcopal Cathedral with its distinctive three spires. Go through the gateposts to the right of the cathedral, keep ahead across the car park and walk to the left of Old Coates House and go right onto the grass to stand outside its doorway.

Old Coates House, also known as Easter Coates House, was built between 1610 and 1615 by John Byres. It was restored in 1830 by Sir Patrick Walker, and later belonged to his daughters Barbara and Mary. The two women never married and bequeathed their entire fortune to the Episcopalian Church on the condition that a cathedral was built on their chosen site. Following the death of the second sister, Mary, in 1870, the bequest was actioned and, following a competition, the job of designing it was given to Sir George Gilbert Scott. The twin smaller spires of the church were completed during World War I and are named for the sisters whose generosity made this glorious church possible.

10 Backtrack to the path, go right then left onto Palmerston Place and then left to enter the cathedral. Once in through the door, go left and on the screen ahead are photographs of Barbara and Mary Walker. Now go along the central aisle, go left in front of the altar and bear right to pass the organ, go up two steps, and the wall on the left is the painting *The Presence*.

It was painted in 1910 by Alfred Edward Borthwick (1871–1955) in 1910 and exhibited throughout Britain, after which it was sent to Germany for copies to be made. But when World War I broke out in 1914 it was illegally sold to an American collector for £5,000. There it would have remained had an American newspaper not used it to illustrate an article entitled 'Is religion dead?'. The paper was sued for breach of copyright and, after the war, an act of Congress was passed to enable the painting to be returned to Scotland. Captain Borthwick gave the painting to the cathedral in 1944 to commemorate the fact that he and his wife had been married here in 1907, and it now hangs alongside a second version of the same title that he painted in 1940.

ST MARY'S CATHEDRAL;

www.cathedral.net

11 Leave the cathedral and go left along Palmerston Place, at the end of which turn left along Atholl Place. Keep ahead over Manor Place and

Coates Crescent, pausing to admire the monumental statue of 19th-century Liberal prime minister William Ewart Gladstone, surrounded by suitably deferential figures. Continue ahead into Shandwick Place, keeping to its left side, and pause outside No. 8, a childhood home of Dr Joseph Bell from 1849 to 1865.

12 Walk to the lights and cross Shandwick Place via the crossing, off which bear left. Keep ahead onto Princes Street and cross over Lothian Street by the crossing. Directly ahead of you is St John's Church.

St John's dates from 1816 and boasts truly magnificent stained-glass windows. Its splendid plaster ceiling vault was inspired by St George's Chapel at Windsor. After exploring the splendid interior of the church, exit and go right and right onto Princes Street, where your walk now comes to an end.

ST JOHN'S CATHEDRAL;

www.stjohns-edinburgh.org.uk

ABOVE: STAINED-GLASS WINDOW IN ST JOHN'S CHURCH, PRINCES STREET

Over Arthur's Seat to Duddingston

This walk combines an ankle-jarring climb over an extinct volcano and a chance to explore one of Edinburgh's most delightful villages.

You might begin this walk with a visit to Holyrood Palace outside of which it starts. Be warned that the first section includes a long climb up the steep, and I do mean steep, slopes of Arthur's Seat, the extinct volcano that looks down on Edinburgh and which is visible from all over the City. On its lower slopes is a very evocative ruined chapel from which stunning views are to be had. A clearly discernible, though in parts uneven, track then climbs towards Arthur's Seat itself. The going can be muddy so sensible footwear is essential. The laborious trudge is well worth it, for once you stand on the rocky summit the views all around will take away what little breath you have left! A gradual descent then brings you to the village of Duddingston, where you can recover your strength at its justifiably famous Sheep Heid Inn, uncover a secret garden, and even climb a loupin-on stane. What's a loupin-on stane? Read on.

1 With your back to the gallery, go left along Horse Wynd and follow the road as it bears left, then right. Go over the car park and cross over the pedestrian crossing, off which bear left. Where the path divides, walk along the cycle route to the left of the 'no entry' sign and keep ahead to go right along the red asphalt path.

Ahead of you is St Margaret's Well. The well house dates from the late 15th century and was moved here in 1860 to be reconstructed over the natural spring.

2 Go to the left of the well and take the grass path that climbs then curves right to bear left along the asphalt path. Just before that path bends sharp right, follow the red earth path that goes straight ahead and climbs between two crags. To your left are the dark waters of St Margaret's Loch.

As the path becomes rocky and uneven and curves uphill, a sequence of rock steps bring you to a circular boulder with a rock basin beneath it. This is St Anthony's Well, which has been dry since the 17th century.

3 Ascend the rocky path to the left of the well, and go left along the earth path that passes between the gorse bushes and brings you to the ruins of St Anthony's Chapel.

An ancient foundation that possibly dates back to before the 1400s, the abbey's history can be read on various boards

WHERE TO EAT

⁜ THE SHEEP HEID INN,
The Causeway, Duddingston;
Tel: 0131 661 7974.
Reputedly Edinburgh's oldest pub and certainly one of its most atmospheric, its walls are adorned with all kinds of famous artefacts. The food is basic pub fare but it is most certainly filling and you couldn't ask for better surroundings in which to recover after traipsing up and over Arthur's Seat. ££

⁜ THE CAFÉ AT HOLYROOD PALACE,
Canongate;
Tel: 0131 556 5100.
Located in the palace's historic Mews Courtyard, the café offers drinks, light snacks and a varied menu of freshly prepared lunches that changes regularly. ££

around the site. This is a lovely spot with magnificent views of Edinburgh and out beyond to the Firth of Forth that stretches beneath you.

4 Backtrack and continue along the path, which divides on reaching a clump of gorse. Take the left pathway, which is virtually straight ahead, and follow the rocky and uneven path. That ascends towards Arthur's Seat and passes to the left of it. Keep climbing until the path plateaus, then take the second path on the right. Keeping to the

DISTANCE **5 miles (8km)**

ALLOW **Approximately 3 hours**

START **Outside the Queen's Gallery Entrance to Holyrood Palace**

FINISH **The main gates of Duddingston Church**

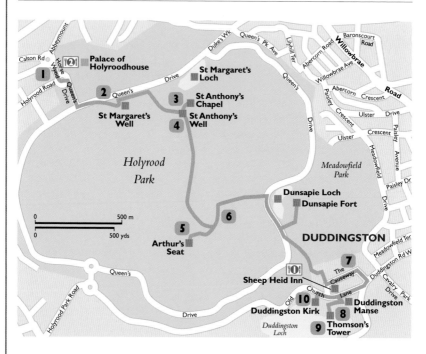

left of the chain fence, continue all the way to the summit. You are standing on the vent of a volcano that last erupted some 350 million years ago. Some claim that its name pertains to the legendary King Arthur, while others claim it is a corruption of 'Archer's Seat', based on the supposition that the rock was a significant defensive point in the Middle Ages. Whatever the origins of its name, the views from this summit are absolutely spectacular and most defininitely reward your trek up.

5 Now begin a descent towards the dark waters of Dunsapie Loch, visible to the left.

In 1836, 17 small wooden coffins were found in a cave just beneath the summit of Arthur's Seat. Each contained a little carved figure. The presumption at the time was that they were in some way connected with witchcraft, although a more recent theory holds that they may have been some form of private memorial to the 17 victims of the

OPPOSITE: SWANS ON DUDDINGSTON LOCH

infamous bodysnatchers Burke and Hare. They are now on display in the National Museum of Scotland on Chambers Street (see Walk 3).

6 When you arrive at a wide grass path go right and follow it to the road. Cross over to the car park, above which on the crag was Dunsapie Fort. Walk diagonally across the car park and take the grass track to the left of the litter bins. You can scramble over the rock to your left to explore the barely visible remnants of the Iron Age fort. Otherwise, keep ahead as the path dips, and at the stone wall go right and descend. Bear left when you meet another path from your right, and go down the steep steps known as Jacob's Ladder. Pass through the hedges, go left through the iron gates and walk between the canyon-like walls to arrive in Duddingston village.

As you emerge on the other side there is a history board on the wall to your left.

Directly ahead of you is the Sheep Heid Inn, Edinburgh's oldest pub, established in 1360, although the current building dates from the 19th century. The sheep's head, eaten boiled or baked, was an old Scottish delicacy and it's from this that the inn's name is believed to be derived. James VI was a frequent visitor and once presented the owner with a silver embossed ram's head. Today it is a lovely and atmospheric old place. In 1728 Maggie Dickson, a Musselburgh-born fishwife, was hanged in Edinburgh for the murder of her illegitimate child. As the body was being taken back to Musselburgh for burial, the entourage stopped for refreshment at the Sheep Heid Inn. They were startled when the corpse suddenly sat up and looked around. She was able to walk home, where she lived out the rest of her days and became something of a local celebrity.

7 Exit the inn, go right and cross to the left side of The Causeway. Follow it as it makes an abrupt right turn, and pause on the left after the long

stone wall outside the white, one-storey cottage, where, on 19 September 1745 Prince Charles Edward Stuart held his decisive council of war before going on to win a major victory at the Battle of Prestonpans. At the end of The Causeway turn right then first right along Old Church Lane. Some way along, go left through the gates of Duddingston Manse, with its mature gardens.

The Manse itself is to the left and over the years has had many famous visitors, including landscape artist J M W Turner and Sir Walter Scott, who reputedly wrote part of *Heart of Midlothian* in the house's garden.

8 Once through the gates, go right along the flagstone path, follow it as it turns left and go through the gate of Dr Neil's Garden, Edinburgh's secret garden. This truly idyllic place was planted by Dr Andrew Neil and his wife Nancy in 1965. Walk down to its left corner and stand on the shores of Duddingston Loch by the tower.

The structure is known as Thomson's Tower after Duddingston Kirk's most famous minister, the landscape painter the Reverend John Thomas (1778–1840). He converted the tower's upper level into a comfortable studio and named it 'Edinburgh', thus enabling his housekeeper to tell parishioners who arrived at the Manse eager for an audience with their minister that he was not available as he had 'gone to Edinburgh'. The view over the Loch,

which has been a bird sanctuary since 1925, is truly inspiring and one can whole-heartedly agree with J M W Turner's comment, when he visited Thomson here, 'By God, sir, I envy you that piece of water'.

9 Backtrack, go out through the gates of the Manse, turn left along Old Church Lane (keeping to its right side), and when you reach the bend, cautiously cross over to see Norman Duddingston Kirk with its unusual tower.

The castellated building to the left of the kirk gates was formerly the watchtower, from which a careful night-time watch was kept over the graves beyond to ensure that a newly buried parishioner would not be dug up and carried off by bodysnatchers. A jougs collar can be seen on wall to the right of the gates. This iron collar and chain was used to punish transgressors for a wide variety of moral offences, including drunkenness, blasphemy, adultery and failing to attend Sunday service. To the right of that is the loupin-on stane, a short flight of rough stone steps surmounted by a platform that was designed to assist old or obese gentlemen to mount and dismount their horses, and to preserve the modesty of ladies struggling to do likewise.

10 Backtrack along the attractive Old Church Lane, go left and cross to the opposite side of the road to reach a bus stop. From here you can take a bus for the quick trip back to the centre of Edinburgh.

A SNOWY SCENE OF ARTHUR'S SEAT AND THE SALISBURY CRAGS

The Ghostly White Lady and a Tragic Witch

Corstorphine is a busy village a short bus ride from the city centre. It is steeped in history and mystery and has several dark tales to chill the blood.

The best days and time to start this walk is on a Wednesday or a Saturday between 10am and noon, when the fascinating little museum run by the Corstorphine Trust is open. However, the rest of the tour can be enjoyed at any time during daylight hours. It begins with a visit to an old medicinal well, and then picks its way through a lovely park to visit a remaining segment of Corstorphine Castle. Taking in the site of a notorious 18th-century murder, the walk then takes you through the delightful village churchyard, where you will discover a very ornate tombstone and hear a tale about supposed witchcraft. Distance-wise this is not a particularly long walk, but the number of interesting sights and site that it encompasses make it a fascinating stroll through a truly historic place.

1 Turn left off the bus, and go right through the gates. Directly ahead of you is the Dower House.

This handsome mid-17th-century dwelling is now the headquarters of the Corstorphine Heritage Trust. It contains a fascinating museum detailing the history of the area.
CORSTORPHINE HERITAGE TRUST;
www.corstorphine-trust.ukgo.com.

2 Exit the gates and go left along Corstorphine High Street. Keep ahead past the bus stop and, as the pavement swerves right then left, you will see a white pebble-dashed building on the left.

This is Claycott House, the oldest house in Corstorphine, where, tradition maintains, Bonnie Prince Charlie's Highland Army rested on 14 September 1745 during the Jacobite uprising.

3 Keep ahead over Ladywell Avenue onto Ladywell Road and, just opposite Ladywell House, go left along Dunsmuir Court. On arrival at the road keep to the left side and follow it downhill. Just past the line of modern houses and flats, cross the green to the bushes and pause by the Physic Well.

Although now covered, you can still see the stone edging that once bordered the well. In the 17th and early 18th centuries the sick would travel many miles to partake of its waters, which were much prized for their medicinal qualities.

4 Backtrack to Ladywell Avenue, go right and keep to the left side. At the iron fence opposite the line of attractive one-storey black and white buildings, go left through the gate into St Margaret's Park. Keep ahead over the grass then turn right along the concrete path to exit the park and go left along Dovecot Road. Keep ahead and, towards its end on the left, is the dovecot.

This is all that now remains of Corstorphine Castle, which was the home of the Forrester lairds from the 14th to the 18th centuries. The doocot was built towards the end of the 16th century and contains 1,060 nest boxes, which would have provided fresh meat for the castle in the winter months and fertilizer for the various crops at other times of the year.

5 Continue along Dovecot Road. In the grounds of 2a, South Lodge, next door, you can see the remains of

OPPOSITE: DOWER HOUSE; ABOVE: DOOCOT (DOVECOT)

DISTANCE 1 mile (1.6km)

ALLOW 1 hour 15 minutes

START Dower House, St Margaret's Park, Corstorphine High Street (bus 1)

FINISH St John's Road

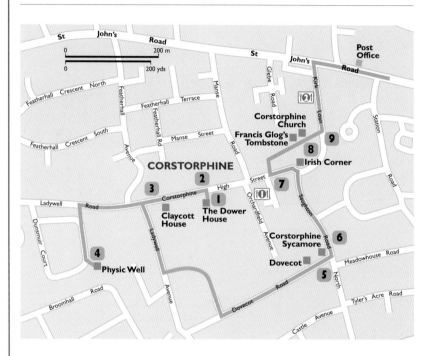

the Corstorphine Sycamore, which stood here for between 400 and 600 years until being blown down by severe winds at 8.10pm on 26 December 1998.

According to tradition, the tree grew from a sapling brought here from the East by a monk. There is also a legend that one of the Forrester lairds buried his jewels and his money beneath the tree. One night a local man arrived here and began digging up the earth. No sooner had he removed his first spade full when a voice

from the ground roared at him to stop what he was doing. The terrified man promptly scurried off into the night. The tree was also the scene of a notorious local murder. In 1679, James Baillie, the 2nd Lord Forrester, was a fervent Presbyterian and an ardent royalist, who was fined £2,500 by Cromwell's Commonwealth. Thereafter he sought solace in drink and embarked upon a stormy affair with an attractive woman named Christian Nimmo, the wife of a wealthy Edinburgh merchant. However, when it transpired

that Christian was in fact the niece of his first wife, Joanna, Baillie promptly terminated the relationship. An enraged Christian arrived in Corstorphine on the night of 26 August 1679, where she learnt that the laird was drinking in his favourite watering hole, The Black Bull. She sent her maid to ask him to meet her and awaited his arrival. The laird arrived drunk and called her a whore, whereupon she snatched his sword from his side and ran him through with it. Baillie fell to the ground and died at the spot. Christian was later found guilty of murder and on 12 November 1679, dressed in a 'whyte taffetie hood' and dress she was beheaded in Edinburgh. However, her ghost, robed in white, still returns to the spot where the murder occurred.

6 Continue and go left along Saughton Road North, where there is a view of the splintered remnants of the sycamore over the wall to your left. Go over Sycamore Gardens and ahead onto Hall Terrace, then left along Corstorphine High Street.

This corner was formerly known as 'Irish Corner' because of the Irish immigrants who lived here, having come to build the Union Canal and then the Edinburgh to Glasgow railway. A red plaque on the wall ahead marks the site of 'Ye Olde Inne – 1561'. This was the Black Bull Inn, where James Baillie enjoyed his last drink on 26 August 1679.

7 Just past the iron railings, very cautiously cross Corstorphine High Street, bear right and go left to pass through two sets of gates into the churchyard. To the left of the second gate you pass a sycamore propagated from a graft taken from the original Corstorphine Sycamore. Cross towards the porch and, just to right of the black bench, pause to examine the curious tombstone of Francis Glog.

Glog, who died in 1738, was the farmer at Claycott, the house you passed earlier in the walk. The carvings on his tombstone are incredibly elaborate and include the head of a Green Man, symbolizing fertility and the cycle of life and death in both man and nature. There are two figures depicting 18th-century farmers sowing and reaping, whilst on the back of the stone is a carving of old

ABOVE: TOMBSTONE OF FRANCIS GLOG

Father Time himself. On 13 May 1649 Beatrix Watson was accused of witchcraft. Giving evidence on oath before the minister and the kirk session, villagers spoke of how they had been struck with mysterious illnesses after angry exchanges with Beatrix. One told of how she had sent his cow into a frenzied state when it had strayed into her yard. Two men claimed that they had been talking to the minister at the back of the churchyard when Beatrix walked by. 'God save the cattle', one exclaimed, and when pressed for an explanation by the minister replied, 'She is not canny. She has the evil eye.' No sooner had the words left his mouth than the oxen had bolted and the two men fell to the ground. James Hadden, Lord Forrester's bailiff, arrested Beatrix and locked her up in the church tower, to await transfer to Edinburgh. The horror of what lay ahead must have terrified the poor woman as she pondered her fate. On the 25 May the bell was heard ringing out from the belfry. When the church officers arrived, they found a terrible sight – Beatrix had hanged herself from the bell rope.

8 Proceed counter-clockwise around the church (the Collegiate Church of St. John the Baptist) and, on arrival at the opposite side, pause to look up above the east window at the light in the niche.

In the Middle Ages Corstorphine was surrounded by marsh and travellers caught out after dark ran the risk of losing their way and even drowning in the numerous bogs. To aid travellers,

the church maintained an oil lamp that burned throughout the night to guide them across the boggy ground towards the safety and the hospitality of the village. The current lamp dates back to 1958 and was placed here by the Corstorphine Rotary. At night its beam shines out from the parish kirk.

9 Continue to the end of the path, go right and exit the churchyard to go left along Kirk Loan. Cross immediately to its right side and, at the end, go right along St John's Road. Keep ahead past the traffic lights and cross the road via the pedestrian traffic lights towards the post office. Bear right and keep ahead to the bus stop, where this walk ends and you can take the bus back to the city centre.

A Blood-soaked Landscape

This is a walk through the beautiful countryside of the Pentland Hills that explores and explains the events of a notorious 17th-century battle.

On 28 November 1666 a well-trained and well-armed government force some 3,000 strong, and under the command of General Tam Dalziel, annihilated a Covenanter force that numbered just 900 at the battle of Rullion Green. This walk explores the tumultuous events of that long-ago day whilst taking in some enchanting scenery that provides a sharp contrast to the turbulent past that this landscape has witnessed. Brooding hills, picturesque glens and babbling burns are your constant companions as you wander along meandering paths, the rush of the modern world falling farther behind with every step you take. In addition to the tale of the battle, you will also visit the remnants of an ancient hill fort before arriving at the monument that marks the burial place for those who fell in the battle. Be warned, however, that sections of the walk can be very muddy, especially after rain, so stout footwear is absolutely essential. Bear in mind also that much of the walk involves steep uphill walking.

1 Walk along the road to the right of the Flotterstone Inn and go into the car park via its second entrance. Bear left and pass the Pentland Hills Ranger Service Countryside Information Centre with exhibitions and events on offer.

It is worth visiting the exhibition here, which displays details on the history, topography and points of interest of the area. Continue ahead onto a path that passes the Flotterstone Sheep Stell, a recreation of one of the drystane structures used for gathering sheep in the hills around you, although this one is for walkers to sit in and relax.

2 Keep going along the path through the gaps in the walls, passing on the right the blue plaque commemorating Professor Colin Thomson Rees Wilson (1869–1959), the distinguished physicist.

The professor, inventor of the Cloud Chamber, was born nearby. His invention enabled him to become the first person to see and photograph the tracks of individual alpha- and beta-particles and electrons in 1911. This important discovery earned him the Nobel Prize for Physics in 1927.

3 Continue along the path that joins the road. Farther along the path go left through the gap in the wall and through a gate (following the sign for Scald Law). Continue, keeping the burn and stone wall to your left. Go left through the gate, again signed Scald Law, and follow the path left to cross the

WHERE TO EAT

IOI THE FLOTTERSTONE INN, Milton Bridge (A702 Biggar Road), Near Penicuik; Tel: 01968 673717.
A pleasant roadside inn that offers a comforting environment in which to sit and contemplate the momentous events you are about to or have encountered. ££

footbridge over Glencorse Burn, off which bear right and begin the ascent of the uneven track. The path rises and passes to the left of a small hillock, then goes over a hill after which it bears right at the fence to get to a gate. Keep ahead through the gate. Pass through another gate, pause and look down across the glen.

This is a beautiful spot to rest and take in the glorious combination of brooding hills, gorgeous countryside and pure, fresh air.

4 Turn left through the gate and trudge up the hill. On arrival at the chained gate, follow the line of the dry stone dyke and keep with it when it bends sharp left.

It was on the slopes to your right that the initial skirmish of the Battle of Rullion Green took place on the 28 November 1666. The battle was the culmination of the Covenanter Pentland Rising that began on 13 November, when four Covenanters, who had been in hiding

OPPOSITE: DRYSTONE DYKE, A STONE WALL AND PURPLE HEATHER

DISTANCE **3.5 miles (6km)**

ALLOW **2 hours 30 minutes–3 hours**

START **Flotterstone Inn, Flotterstone on the A702 (bus 93, 100, 101 or 102)**

FINISH **Flotterstone Inn**

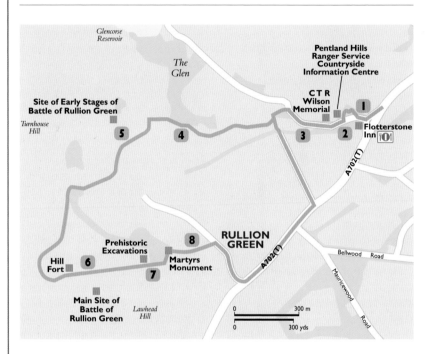

close to Loch Ken in Galloway, came to the aid of an old man who was about to be tortured by a group of government troops for refusing to pay his fine for non-attendance at church. With the rising underway, a Covenanter force, some 180 strong, marched on Dumfries and took prisoner Sir James Turner, a professional soldier who had been tasked by the government with suppressing the Covenanter movement. Nine hundred rebels led by Captain James Wallace then marched for Edinburgh, at which point

a well-armed government force of 3,000 set out in pursuit under the command of the notorious general Tam Dalziel, the commander of the King's forces in Scotland. When the insurgents reached Colinton, to the west of Edinburgh, the weather began to deteriorate appallingly, and Wallace, having suffered a number of desertions, decided to retreat southwards. Dalziel moved quickly to block his retreat and, as sunset approached on 28 November, an advance group of 22 government cavalry caught up with,

OPPOSITE: A STREAM TRICKLES THROUGH THE GREEN COUNTRYSIDE OF FLOTTERSTONE

attacked and were repulsed by 80 insurgents on the slopes of Turnhouse Hill to the right.

5 Follow the dry stone dyke and, having passed to the right of a gate, keep the fence to your left, and head for the right side of the long line of trees to the left in the distance. Having passed the trees, veer sharp left and follow the dry stone wall, until you come to a crater-like depression in the ground. At this point turn right, passing to the right side of the depression and ascend diagonally left towards the fence, on

arrival at which turn right and follow it to pass through the metal gate. Turn left and walk to the summit of the hill ahead, noting the ramparts of a prehistoric hill fort that are cut into the hillock.

At the summit pause and look across at the hill opposite, crowned by three radio masts. This is Lawhead Hill and it was in the hollow below you that the main encounter of the Battle of Rullion Green occurred. As darkness fell, the Covenanters, who had the advantage of higher ground, managed to resist two attacks by Dalziel's infantry and cavalry,

ABOVE: MARTYRS MEMORIAL

but they were routed by the third sally, and 50 of them were killed on the battlefield. As the fray drew to a close, Dalziel recognized Captain John Paton, who had fought beside him at the battle of Worcester in 1651 but was now on the opposing side, leaving the field. According to Robert Louis Stevenson, Dalziel was 'determined to capture him with his own hands…and charged forward, presenting his pistols. Paton fired, but the balls hopped off Dalziel's buff coat and fell into his boot. With the superstition peculiar to his age, the Nonconformist concluded that his adversary was rendered bullet-proof by enchantment, and, pulling some small silver coins from his pocket, charged his pistol therewith. Dalziel, seeing this, and supposing, it is likely, that Paton was putting in larger balls, hid behind his servant, who was killed'. The battle over, the survivors fled into the darkness with the government troops in hot pursuit. A hundred Covenanters were captured, 30 of whom were taken to Edinburgh, where they were either suffered the fate of being hanged for treason and rebellion or transported to Barbados.

6 Having pondered those long-ago events, descend towards the gate and trees that are clearly visible to your left. Go through the gate and walk towards the right corner of the trees directly ahead.

Just before you arrive at them you will notice a series of depressions in the ground. These were excavated between 1983 and 1985 and small deposits of cremated bones were uncovered, which were dated to between 600 and 100BC.

7 Go through the gate to the right of the trees, and descend the path that runs between the plantation and the wall. Pass through the next gate, turn immediately left and a little way along on the left pause alongside the blood red railings that surround the Martyrs Monument to contemplate their fate.

This marks the grave of the 50 Covenanters who died at the Battle of Rullion Green. A history of the monument can be read on the plaque fixed to the railings.

8 Descend to the left across the field towards Rullion Green Cottage, exit through the gate to the right of the green shed and, at the end of the driveway, go left along the main road. Follow the pavement as it veers left, then go left along the path signed Glencorse Reservoir. Keep ahead until it bends left, at which point keep straight ahead through the wooden gate. When the path swings left and descends steeply, head for the bridge to the right, cross it and go out through the gate. Veer right, and keep ahead along the path to pass through the next gate and, having stepped through the gap in the wall, turn right along the road and follow it back to the Flotterstone Inn.

Once past the inn go left along the A702 to the bus stop from where you can take a bus back to Edinburgh.

INDEX

ACKNOWLEDGEMENTS

The Automobile Association would like to thank the following photographers, companies and picture libraries for their assistance in the preparation of this book.

Abbreviations for the picture credits are as follows: (AA) AA World Travel Library.

Front Cover: Scottish Viewpoint/Alamy; 3 Edinburgh Inspiring Capital, www.edinburgh-inspiringcapital.com; 7 Scottish Viewpoint/Alamy; 8 AA/R Elliot; 11 Edinburgh Inspiring Capital, www.edinburgh-inspiringcapital.com; 13 AA/J Smith; 14 © Jean-Christophe Godet / Alamy; 15 AA/J Smith; 18 © Duncan Hale-Sutton / Alamy; 20/21 AA/K Paterson; 22 Edinburgh Inspiring Capital, www.edinburgh-inspiringcapital.com; 23 AA/S Whitehorne; 26 Edinburgh Inspiring Capital, www.edinburgh-inspiringcapital.com; 28 AA/J Smith; 31 The Real Mary King's Close; 32 AA/K Paterson; 34/35 AA/K Paterson; 36 Edinburgh Inspiring Capital, www.edinburgh-inspiringcapital.com; 39 © Jean-Christophe Godet / Alamy; 40 Edinburgh Inspiring Capital, www.edinburgh-inspiringcapital.com; 42 Edinburgh Inspiring Capital, www.edinburgh-inspiringcapital.com; 45 Edinburgh Inspiring Capital, www.edinburgh-inspiringcapital.com; 46 © doughoughton / Alamy; 48/49 Edinburgh Inspiring Capital, www.edinburgh-inspiringcapital.com; 50 The Royal College of Surgeons of Edinburgh; 53 © Jean-Christophe Godet / Alamy; 55 The Royal College of Surgeons of Edinburgh; 56 Robin Gauldie; 59 Robin Gauldie; 60 Robin Gauldie; 61 Robin Gauldie; 62/63 Edinburgh Inspiring Capital, www.edinburgh-inspiringcapital.com; 64 Edinburgh Inspiring Capital, www.edinburgh-inspiringcapital.com; 65 Edinburgh Inspiring Capital, www.edinburgh-inspiringcapital.com; 67 Edinburgh Inspiring Capital, www.edinburgh-inspiringcapital.com; 68 AA; 70 AA/D Corrance; 71 AA/K Paterson; 73 © Duncan Hale-Sutton / Alamy; 74 © Duncan Hale-Sutton / Alamy; 76/77 AA/J Smith; 78 © inspirepix / Alamy; 82 AA/S Whitehorne; 83 © Duncan Hale-Sutton / Alamy; 84 © Malcolm Fife / Alamy; 87 © Marco Secchi / Alamy; 88/89 © Jason Baxter / Alamy; 90/91 AA/K Paterson; 92 Isla Love; 95 AA/K Paterson; 97 AA/D Corrance; 98 © David Kilpatrick / Alamy; 99 © Duncan Hale-Sutton / Alamy; 100 © Paul Bock / Alamy; 103 © PCL / Alamy; 105 © David Robertson / Alamy; 106 © doughoughton / Alamy; 109 AA/J Smith; 110 AA/J Smith; 112/113 AA/J Smith; 114 Richard Jones; 117 © Don Brownlow / Alamy; 119 Richard Jones; 120 AA/M Alexander; 124 © Ros Drinkwater / Alamy; 126/127 AA/R Elliot; 128 AA/K Paterson; 129 AA/D Corrance; 133 © seasonalpik / Alamy; 134 © StockImages / Alamy; 137 Isla Love; 138 AA/K Paterson; 140 © Duncan Hale-Sutton / Alamy; 142 © Bernd Mellmann / Alamy; 144/145 © Stewart Bremner / Alamy; 146 © Rough Guides / Alamy; 147 © 197 aerial photography / Alamy; 148 AA/K Paterson; 151 AA/J Smith; 153 © inspirepix / Alamy; 154 Edinburgh Inspiring Capital, www.edinburgh-inspiringcapital.com; 157 Edinburgh Inspiring Capital, www.edinburgh-inspiringcapital.com; 158 Edinburgh Inspiring Capital, www.edinburgh-inspiringcapital.com; 160/161 Edinburgh Inspiring Capital, www.edinburgh-inspiringcapital.com; 162 Robin Gauldie; 163 Richard Jones; 165 Robin Gauldie; 166 Richard Jones; 168 AA/E Ellington; 171 AA/K Paterson; 172 Richard Jones

Every effort has been made to trace the copyright holders, and we apologize in advance for any accidental errors. We would be happy to apply the corrections in the following edition of this publication.